RAW

basics

ALSO BY JENNY ROSS

*THE ART OF RAW LIVING FOOD: Heal Yourself and
the Planet with Eco-delicious Cuisine* (with Doreen Virtue)

HAY HOUSE TITLES OF RELATED INTEREST

YOU CAN HEAL YOUR LIFE, the movie,
starring Louise L. Hay & Friends
(available as a 1-DVD program and an expanded 2-DVD set)
Watch the trailer at: **www.LouiseHayMovie.com**

THE SHIFT, the movie, starring Dr. Wayne W. Dyer
(available as a 1-DVD program and an expanded 2-DVD set)
Watch the trailer at: **www.DyerMovie.com**

THE BELLY FAT CURE: Discover the New Carb Swap System™
and Lose 4 to 9 lbs. Every Week, by Jorge Cruise

*HEALTH BLISS: 50 Revitalizing NatureFoods & Lifestyle Choices
to Promote Vibrant Health,* by Susan Smith Jones, Ph.D.

*VEGETARIAN MEALS FOR PEOPLE-ON-THE-GO:
101 Quick & Easy Recipes,* by Vimala Rodgers

*THE YO-YO DIET SYNDROME: How to Heal and
Stabilize Your Appetite and Weight,* by Doreen Virtue

All of the above are available at your
local bookstore, or may be ordered by visiting:

Hay House USA: **www.hayhouse.com**®
Hay House Australia: **www.hayhouse.com.au**
Hay House UK: **www.hayhouse.co.uk**
Hay House South Africa: **www.hayhouse.co.za**
Hay House India: **www.hayhouse.co.in**

JENNY ROSS

RAW
basics

Incorporating Raw Living Foods
into Your Diet Using Easy
and Delicious Recipes

HAY HOUSE, INC.
Carlsbad, California • New York City
London • Sydney • Johannesburg
Vancouver • Hong Kong • New Delhi

Published and distributed in the United States by: Hay House, Inc.: www.hayhouse.com • *Published and distributed in Australia by:* Hay House Australia Pty. Ltd.: www.hayhouse.com .au • *Published and distributed in the United Kingdom by:* Hay House UK, Ltd.: www.hayhouse .co.uk • *Published and distributed in the Republic of South Africa by:* Hay House SA (Pty), Ltd.: www .hayhouse.co.za • *Distributed in Canada by:* Raincoast: www.raincoast.com • *Published in India by:* Hay House Publishers India: www.hayhouse.co.in

Editorial supervision: Jill Kramer • *Project editor:* Alex Freemon
Cover design: Christy Salinas • *Interior design:* Tricia Breidenthal
Main recipe photos: Kit Chan, Fringe Photography, and Lyle Okihara
Additional photos: Dreamstime and Shutterstock

Library of Congress Cataloging-in-Publication Data

Ross, Jenny.
    Raw basics : incorporating raw living foods into your diet using easy and delicious recipes / Jenny Ross.
        p. cm.
    Includes bibliographical references.
    ISBN 978-1-4019-3166-7 (hardback)
    1. Natural foods. 2. Raw foods. 3. Raw food diet. I. Title.
    TX369.R667 2011
    641.3'02--dc22

                                                    2010052865

Hardcover ISBN: 978-1-4019-3166-7
Digital ISBN: 978-1-4019-3167-4

14 13 12 11   4 3 2 1
1st edition, July 2011

Printed in China

For Grandma Ross, thanks for "playing restaurant" with me all those years and teaching me how to have fun, even with the hard stuff.

To my parents, Tamara and Charles, thank you for helping me pursue my passion at every turn and supporting my ever-evolving process; to Aunt Jerrie and Uncle Dennis, for teaching me what unconditional love looks like; and to my son, Dylan, for bringing me and our family "back to the basics" in such a beautiful way. I love you.

To the entire team at 118 Degrees, thanks for your continued support of our vision to "educate the world about the power of gourmet living foods." Your hard work and efforts have helped shape the lives of so many people.

CONTENTS

$\mathcal{I}$NTRODUCTION

Ten years ago, my personal journey with living foods began. As I changed my life-style, eating choices, and personal way of working with and looking at food, I arrived at such a euphoric place of good health that I wanted to shout about it from the rooftops. I became very passionate about sharing the wellness and vitality I was now living with the world. Of course, I knew nothing of how this would unfold except that I was com-mitted to making a difference.

As my personal journey has evolved, I have been blessed with the opportunity to spread the word about living foods to more and more people, one day at a time. Through my current restaurant, 118 Degrees, in Costa Mesa, California; workshops and classes; and hands-on educational experiences, I've been a part of bringing this powerful lifestyle to more than 100,000 people, and have seen truly miraculous things.

Whenever I teach, and oftentimes in the restaurant, customers will ask me, "What is the easiest way to start 'doing' raw foods?" Of course, there is no magic an-swer or a one-size-fits-all approach to embarking on the path of living foods, but there *are* some basics that can help even the most novice cooks begin creating healthy and delicious raw dishes they will love.

Raw Basics is designed to answer this important question, as well as inspire you to begin adding more fresh, vibrant foods to your diet. We have a saying at 118 that goes like this: "Just start adding more of the good stuff." I've found that more than 80 percent of our clients get great results if they begin by focusing on *adding* to their diet. Adding, not subtracting. As they shift to learning great raw options and incorporating them into their everyday eating, the other foods they've been trying to give up just sort of fall away, leaving them feeling refreshed and invigorated.

Enjoy this book as a whole, or skip to the recipes that sound good to you, and actively explore each section on its own. In a very fundamental way, this book is designed to educate and empower you so you can find a healthy balance in your diet . . . leading to vibrant health!

HOW MUCH LIVING FOOD DOES THE BODY NEED?

It's true that every little bit of raw food you add to your diet counts, and at the end of just a week, you'll feel more vibrant and alive. Living bodies need living food: the idea is that for everything you add to your life, you get more of the same. Negative thoughts breed negativity. Foods that are devoid of life and life-enhancing agents foster death and disease. For every "nonvital" part of your diet that you replace with something vital to your overall health, you become "more of" health.

Our bodies serve our minds and souls to the utmost when in good physical condition; and we are "more of" who we are and can therefore offer more to the world, those around us, our work, and our lives. When our bodies do not serve us and our health is failing, there is "more of" disease, and we must work to restore the balance of wellness that is our birthright as human beings. We were designed to embody optimal health!

IS "RAW FOODS" A DIET FAD?

The answer to the above question is no. The living-foods diet does more than restrict calories, speed metabolism, and shrink fat cells. It is a *lifestyle*—one that brings about health and restores balance. This balanced functioning allows the body to fight disease properly and nourish itself while performing vital operations that keep you youthful and energetic.

RAW basics

The number one reason many diets fail is because they are too restrictive in the minds of the dieters. You can get around this by eliminating the *need* to diet, instead choosing nourishing substances like raw whole foods, and adjusting the mental focus in the process from what you can't have to what you *get* to have. This is a basic and positive "recipe" for success.

I observed a client (whom I was fortunate enough to share the living-foods lifestyle with) really struggling in the early days of trying to release old habits during her transition to a more whole-foods-based diet. So I asked her, "What foods do you think about?"

She replied, "Everything I can't have."

"What makes you think you can't have them?" I asked her.

She looked at me, shocked, and said, "Well, they're not good for me!"

I smiled and said, "So you are *choosing* not to have them, because your vibrant health is more important to you, right?"

And she replied simply, "Yes," followed by a sigh of relief.

When you're strong enough to choose more of the good stuff, the focus is different: it's about taking a proactive approach to your goals. Then you can explore. You can literally play like a child would, discovering new things that will catapult your health in ways you could never imagine.

ARE THE NEGATIVE EFFECTS OF PAST PHYSICAL DAMAGE REVERSIBLE?

Health is cumulative, and the best preventive medicine I know of is to treat your body well. Over the past decade, I have seen it time and time again: customers—ones who thought optimal health could never be reached again in their lifetime—focus on adding more raw food to their meals and begin reversing diseases that have plagued them for years.

One of the most immediately rewarding ways to begin to treat your body better is to eliminate toxins from your diet. Forgoing cooked oils and greasy, fried foods is a great place to start; and cutting back on animal products and focusing on plant-based cuisine provides a wonderful foundation for health.

Of course, eliminating processed foods from your diet will yield tremendous and tangible results. These benefits include weight loss, increased energy, lower cholesterol, healthy blood pressure, physical endurance, glowing skin, renewed hair growth, mental clarity . . . and countless others.

"Let your food
be your medicine,
your medicine food."

— HIPPOCRATES

WHAT IS THE LIVING-FOODS LIFESTYLE?

Living or "raw" foods are those that have not been heated above 118 degrees Fahrenheit. This is the commonly agreed-upon temperature after which plant-based ingredients begin to break down and lose essential vitamin and mineral content, as well as enzymes. Pure and simple, raw foods are natural foods in their natural state. In addition to breaking down enzymes and nutrients, many modern-day cooking methods actually create by-products during the heating process that have been found to be toxic.

Raw foods are primarily plant based. Fruits, vegetables, nuts, seeds, and sprouted grains are the basis of this culinary lifestyle. In addition, living-foods enthusiasts oftentimes make use of high-grade minerals and other superfoods as a way of restoring balance. Juicing is an effective alternative-health remedy and is currently being used in several cancer-treatment centers worldwide, with incredible life-enhancing results. A high-nutrient-density diet goes a long way toward maintaining overall health, and living foods are at the top of the scale in terms of nutrient density and purity.

Living foods are not a new idea; in fact, many would counter that this is the *oldest* notion of how to eat. The Bible contains several references to living-food preparations; early texts discuss the heating of plant-based ingredients and "cooking" using the energy of the sun. In many ancient cultures where longevity of life was enjoyed, there was also a focus on fresh, living foods.

This style of eating can help you reach and maintain your health goals, for three main reasons:

1. The living-foods lifestyle encourages a very low-toxin diet, with a focus on the function of every food and how it is helping you achieve health. With living foods, there are simply no fillers, artificial preservatives, or unneeded additives that do not benefit your body in some way. As a result, the living-foods diet is largely alkaline forming. Disease cannot live in an alkaline environment; it must have a toxic, acidic one to thrive. Picture the pH test strips from your high-school chemistry class. On the pH scale, 14 is totally alkaline, 7 is neutral, and 0–6 is acidic. The body should be anywhere from neutral to moderately alkaline to prevent disease.

2. Raw foods constitute a plant-based diet, which has been proven to maintain strong vital organs and optimal bodily function. Overall health has been shown to drastically improve in direct relationship to how much plant-based eating you're doing. From providing essential proteins, amino acids, minerals, and vitamins to detoxifying the body where necessary, this eating style serves to keep you in balance.

3. Living foods have the power to heal the body by reintroducing essential vitamins and minerals, as well as enzymes—the catalysts that break down nutrients into a usable state. With a diet rich in enzymes, your body isn't overwhelmed with the breaking-down process (called *assimilation*) and has time then to go about the business of maintaining a vital system and promoting health.

Whether you're looking to move into a more energetic space, restore overall wellness, achieve a vibrant lifestyle, or find alternatives to processed foods and their associated health conditions (ulcers, indigestion, headaches, chronic fatigue, and depression have all been linked to poor diet), living foods could prove to be a very viable option for you . . . and even serve to heal you completely.

Trying the living-foods lifestyle, even if for only one day or one meal a week, will start to give you an idea of what is possible. Keep in mind that this is not an all-or-nothing proposition. Choosing to add even one more component of living nutrition to your daily eating plan will begin the process. The best choice you can make for the health of your body and mind is to take control of your diet one bite at a time. Go back to the basics of health, and add in more of the good stuff.

WHAT IS THE GOOD STUFF?

No matter what your current diet, it's easier to add something new—more of the good stuff—instead of being focused on what to take away. Deciding which items are right for your body or are important for nutrition can be a challenge. Here is a list of questions to consider when evaluating whether a food selection really constitutes the "good stuff":

- Where did this food come from?

- Can it grow from the ground? (Picture a tree full of cheese puffs or Oreo cookies and you're on the right track.)

- What is the health benefit of eating this?

- How was this food prepared?

The golden rule in choosing good, nourishing food is finding items that are *local, fresh, organic* (without pesticides), and *grown from a healthy vital plant* of some sort. In general, this includes all fruits and vegetables in their natural state, nuts and seeds, grains, herbs and spices, superfoods, and products minimally processed from any of the above-listed items. These are all whole foods.

A nice raw nut, for example, makes a fantastic raw butter. But if you roast nuts, then add iodized salt and some preservatives, you've just created a product that could very well be hazardous to your health. The average jar of peanut butter contains unhealthy levels of saturated fats and iodine, along with bleached white salts that are toxic in the bloodstream.

Really, what you have to consider when making choices at the grocery store are the following questions:

1. **What is the food product itself?** It should be fresh, organic wherever possible, and from a plant source. Tomatoes and avocados are perfect examples of fresh, whole foods.

2. **How has it been treated?** If it has been cooked, there could now be many toxins entering into the picture. To make a cooked product shelf stable, a preservative of some sort typically must be added. Preservatives act the same way in the body as they do in the food itself and can be easily stored for years, blocking your absorption of important nutrients, until released during a cleansing process. So although a tomato is a good choice, tomato sauce in a can is probably not. The can contains harmful

metals, and the contents have been processed and may include up to 14 different un-natural ingredients just to increase shelf life. Look into the ingredients list, and also the processing. If it's not very "vibrant," then it does not equate to vibrant health for you!

3. Where does it come from? Processed crackers, for example, come from a box with a side label that lists 10 to 20 ingredients you may have never heard of before (enriched flours, dioxides, and so on). Bags of potato chips line the shelves, and while it is very tempting to reason that a potato once came from the earth and is therefore "natural," don't take the bait. You know that fried oils are *not* natural; that ground potato flakes, which are the starter for many brands of commercial chips, are treated with chemicals to alter how they look; and that preserving agents are anything but wholesome.

4. What are its health benefits? Food should taste great, but it should also be functional. Ask yourself what you're getting out of every bite. Food is fuel; you want top-notch ingredients for top-notch performance.

Raw-Foods Shopping List

Here is my go-to shopping list for the basics to stock a kitchen full of living foods.

— *Fresh produce.* Shopping organic and local wherever possible is the best choice for your health.

- **Apples and pears**: When in season, these fruits make a great base for many recipes and can be used in sweet and savory dishes.
- **Avocados (Hass and Reed):** Make sure avocados are somewhat soft and haven't been picked too early. Those that are hard when picked may not ripen, especially early and late in the season.
- **Citrus**: Oranges, lemons, limes, and grapefruit act as solvents, which are good for cleaning the liver and gallbladder. Lemons are used in place of vinegar in many recipes in this book.
- **Dark, leafy greens**: Kale, collard greens, spinach, and red and green chard provide necessary protein and chlorophyll. Our cousins the apes enjoy a diet that is over 40 percent dark, leafy greens. Greens help build muscle and connective tissue.

- **Heirloom tomatoes, Roma tomatoes, or fresh tomatoes from the vine:** Tomatoes are best when in season and sourced locally. Heirloom varieties come in many different colors and shapes, and the benefit of enjoying these in season is a much higher nutrient density, because the seeds haven't been hybridized or genetically altered over time to create stronger crops.

- **Fresh herbs:** Basil, cilantro, and green onions are my standbys for stocking the fridge. Store these wrapped in a wet cloth or inside a small bottle of water to keep them fresh.

- **Fresh berries:** Berries are a heavily sprayed crop, so it's very important to shop for organic or pesticide-free selections wherever possible. If you must buy conventional produce, be sure to rinse the berries well with a vegetable wash to remove any residue.

- **Zucchini or yellow squash:** Squash is a very mineral-dense row crop and is typically easy to find. The water content makes it readily digested, and it's a great base for many vegetable dishes.

- **Garlic:** Garlic is an immunity-boosting ingredient that is also good for heart function. It contrasts with other flavors for a superior culinary experience.

- **Young Thai coconuts:** Young Thai coconuts yield 1–2 cups of coconut water each, as well as up to a cup of coconut flesh.

- **Bananas:** Bananas are a great base for smoothies, and are high in potassium.

- **Shiitake or portobello mushrooms:** Mushrooms are great to have in the kitchen year-round and are very powerful during cold-and-flu season to boost immunity.

— **Nuts, seeds, and grains.** Shop for raw, unpasteurized, and unheated varieties. Be sure to store in a cool, dark space to protect the integrity of the oils present in the nuts. Soaking and sprouting your raw nuts and seeds is recommended as you begin to add more to your diet. This process releases the enzyme inhibitor naturally present within the nut, activating it to make the nutrients more readily available for digestion. The amount of soaking time varies per nut.

- **Raw tahini (ground sesame seeds):** This is actually pretty hard to make at home and worth buying jarred when you can. (Artisana is my favorite brand!) Tahini is high in calcium and B vitamins, and is an easy ingredient to whip into sauces and spreads in a hurry.

- **Miso:** Shop for a mellow white miso that is unpasteurized, or a brown or red variety for more flavor. Make sure it is labeled "non-GMO," as many soy crops are genetically modified.

- **Raw almond butter and raw almonds:** Almonds are one of the only nuts that are naturally alkaline forming. Raw almond butter is a great substitute for peanut butter.

- **Raw flaxseed:** Flax is rich in essential fatty acids such as omega-3 and omega-6, as well as fiber. A great base for wraps and crackers, flaxseed is helpful for optimal digestion and brain function.

- **Macadamia nuts:** Naturally creamy, macadamia nuts are a go-to ingredient for making great nut cheeses and yummy sauces. The essential fatty acids are incredible for promoting healthy hair, glowing skin, and elastic nails. *Soak time:* 4 hours.

- **Pistachios:** Pistachios whip up into a great pesto and are easy to store. Shop for raw varieties—unsalted, out of the shell. *Soak time:* 4 hours.

- **Pecans or walnuts:** These nuts have naturally occurring oil that makes a great component for many desserts. Try to keep one or the other on hand at all times. *Soak time:* 4 hours.

- **Pumpkin seeds:** Pumpkin seeds offer superior health benefits to sunflower seeds and have a great flavor to work with on a culinary level. *Soak time:* 6 hours.

- **Quinoa:** A gluten-free seed, high in protein, quinoa (pronounced "kee-NO-wah") is a natural alternative to wheat and rice. *Soak time:* 12 hours.

- **Kamut or rye berries:** Kamut is a high-protein grain; when sprouted, it contains only trace amounts of gluten. This is a nonhybridized heirloom grain indigenous to Egypt. Rye also has a small amount of gluten—but less than wheat—and is known to be high in protein, magnesium, and calcium. *Soak time:* 12 hours, followed by 2–3 days for sprouting.

- **Raw buckwheat:** Buckwheat is a gluten-free grain with a high protein profile. Fast and easy to sprout, it is an important ingredient if you love crunchy foods, as it dries to a very crispy texture. *Soak time:* 12 hours.

— ***Basic pantry.*** These items can keep in your pantry indefinitely.

- **Olives:** Look for kalamata, green, or sun-dried black varieties; these should be packaged dry or in oil, not in vinegar or with additional salt.

- **Dulse and other raw sea vegetables:** Maine Coast Sea Vegetables are hand-harvested and sun-dried. Look for purple colors and wild varieties. Dulse is easily integrated into many recipes.

- **Raw honey or agave nectar:** To find the best raw honey (which helps fight allergies), I suggest seeking out your local beekeeper. When shopping for agave, look for a dark color, and make sure it's labeled "raw."

- **Raw cacao, maca-root powder, and supergreens:** These supplements can be a daily smoothie staple and provide needed minerals. Superfoods are generally found in the supplement section of your local health-food store and online. (See additional superfood suggestions in Chapter 3.)

- **Raw coconut aminos:** This great substitute for soy sauce is soy and wheat free.

- **Sun-dried tomatoes:** Look for unsalted varieties, oftentimes packed in olive oil.

- **Shredded coconut:** Be sure to buy dried coconut shreds that are unsweetened and unsulfured.

- **Assorted chili peppers:** Naturally dried peppers are the best in terms of taste and health benefits. Chipotle peppers are naturally smoked and create a great flavor in sauces and spreads.

- **Dried figs:** Look for unsulfured and sun-dried mission figs for use in the recipes in this book.

- **Himalayan and other gourmet salts:** Salt should always be a dingy-gray or pink color, as opposed to bright white. (There are also black and red varieties.) It is important to find a great one that hasn't been processed to remove its mineral content. Salt "separates" flavor when creating culinary treats and is an important ingredient in your kitchen. The right salts are also functional because they double as trace-mineral supplements.

- **Cold-pressed extra-virgin olive oil:** Olive oils need to be stored in dark glass to prevent oxidizing. Try many in the "cold-pressed extra-virgin" category until you find one you love the taste of. Since you're not heating the oil, the final flavor profile in many of your dressings and sauces will directly result from it.

- **Truffle-infused oil and other gourmet oils:** These should be used sparingly, but can add a quick and easy burst of flavor. Be sure to look for natural infused oils, not synthetic flavors.

HOW TO SET UP YOUR KITCHEN FOR SUCCESS

Setting up your kitchen for success can be as easy as finding a great functional knife and a cutting board. However, if you plan to jump into the living-foods lifestyle, either in steps or with both feet right away, there are some tools that can help ease the transition.

Introduction to the Tools

- **High-powered blender:** A high-powered blender makes manipulating nuts, seeds, and whole fruits and vegetables fast and easy. I suggest outfitting your kitchen with a blender that has a high and low setting, plus a variable-speed dial for even more ease of use. A plunger is also standard on many of these models and helps blend thick sauces made with nuts and seeds. Without a high-powered blender, living cuisine is still possible, but you *will* need a blender of some sort to create sauces, spreads, and smoothies. I recommend dividing the recipes in half for use in a basic blender to make them easier on the machine.

- **Mandoline:** A mandoline is the tool used to create pastas and layered vegetable dishes. Shop for one that has comfortable grips on the bottom designed to keep the equipment in place during use and that features a rotating blade for easy cleaning.

- **Food processor:** Food processors are used mostly for breads and dough, as well as spreads. A basic model will work in your living-foods kitchen to create all of the dishes in this book.

- **Juicer:** Juicers are nice to have on hand if "cleansing" will be part of your health regimen. You may elect to shop for a machine that helps reduce oxidizing and "extracts" the juice to maintain its integrity. The Green Star Elite, for example, extracts juice through a magnetic field, helping maintain its structure, and therefore the longevity of the juice is extended up to three days.

- **Chef's knife:** Knives that are ceramic will reduce oxidation of the fruits and vegetables, and will maintain a sharp edge much longer than a stainless-steel blade. It's important to find a knife that suits your hand well, as it will be the most-used tool in your kitchen.

- **Cutting board:** Anything on your cutting board will get into your final food product. For this reason, a natural-grain board like bamboo or olive wood is preferred. Make sure to find one that's big enough for your large projects so you have space to maneuver.

- **Glass containers for storage:** Storage containers should be glass to avoid any off-gassing of plastics while your foods are stored. Look for ones with a BPA-free, tight-fitting plastic lid.

- **Glass bowls:** Tossing your salads and vegetables in a glass bowl makes the mixture easier to see and is also preferable for health reasons.

- **Squeeze bottles:** Squeeze bottles are great for storage of sauces for use throughout the week. Look for a set of bottles with BPA-free plastic at your local kitchen store.

- **Dehydrator:** A dehydrator is not essential to a living-foods kitchen, but it really expands what is possible in terms of creating new textures and flavors. This is a logical step if you're adopting living foods as a lifestyle. Shop for a dehydrator like the Sedona by Tribest, which has multiple trays, is square, and utilizes a fan. Dehydrators simulate the natural properties of the sun and wind by moving warm air over the food product to remove moisture, leaving behind essential nutrients, fibers, and intensified flavors.

Before we jump into raw-foods recipes, I'll leave you with three suggestions for success in your kitchen that I recommend for anyone just starting out:

1. Place great food options so that they are readily available throughout the kitchen. A platter of fruit on the countertop or terrific raw cookies next to the refrigerator will always divert the wandering eye and stomach to something healthy.

2. Get set up with great tools that make creating living-foods dishes fun and easy. The more you can equip your kitchen with the right tools, the more likely you are to use the skills you learn. Also, keep the equipment out where you can see it; this is more of a motivator to create fresh foods in your home instead of dining out.

3. Enter with a great attitude! Make your kitchen somewhere fun to be. I have quotes and pictures of people I love in mine, and in my mind I make sure to frame my time there as playtime. This will move you away from the restrictive nature of a diet regimen and into a more permanent lifestyle shift.

"The journey of a thousand miles begins with one step."

— LAO-TZU

$\mathcal{G}$ETTING
STARTED WITH
LIVING FOODS

Let's jump right into some great recipes that you can use every day—multiple times a day, in fact—so you can get started enjoying more raw living foods in your diet. When I started out with this lifestyle, I was literally handed a book by my friend the surfing legend John Peck. John knew I was on a journey looking for health and vitality, and he was acquainted with David Jubb, a noted expert on health with a doctorate in physiology. He sent me Dr. Jubb's book *LifeFood Recipe Book* (co-authored with Annie Jubb), and I read it cover to cover overnight.

The idea presented was so compelling: eat natural food, in its natural state, and experience great health, free from disease and stress. I thought, *Sign me up for that!* So I jumped right in. What was the worst that could happen? I could go back to eating cooked food, no problem—I'd been doing that my whole life and getting horrible results. I encouraged myself to try something new . . . and I hope you will, too!

Please note: Throughout the following chapters, ingredients that appear in bold-face type refer to recipes listed elsewhere in the book. Consult the Recipe Index at the back of the book to locate the pages where instructions for preparing these ingredients can be found.

5 Easy Recipes to Get You Started

"Easy" by definition means that these recipes will take you very little time, require minimal equipment, and also be basic in nature, needing only a few ingredients. Each recipe is also functional, providing important vitamins, minerals, and other essentials for daily nutrition.

RAW basics

HEMP MILK

This is a surprisingly easy recipe, enjoyed by children and adults alike. High in omega-3 and omega-6, as well as chlorophyll, hemp seeds require no advance soaking to derive optimal nutritional benefit.

2 cups hemp seeds

2 cups purified water

2 Tbsp. raw sweetener (raw honey or agave nectar)

1 dash sea salt

Cinnamon, nutmeg, or vanilla as desired (optional)

In a basic blender, combine all required ingredients and blend well. You should quickly notice a rich, creamy white milk form. Pour the mixture through a strainer into a cup to remove any husk residue. If stored properly in the refrigerator, this milk can be kept for the next 4–5 days for use in cereals, in smoothies, and as a delicious afternoon snack. To give your milk some zest, try adding 1 tsp. cinnamon, 1 dash nutmeg, and 1 tsp. vanilla bean or vanilla-bean flavoring.

If you're low on hemp seeds, another quick fix for milk is to use nut butter. Coconut is actually my favorite, but you can substitute 4 Tbsp. of any type of raw nut butter in the above recipe and get the same results. It works well with raw almond, pecan, and walnut butter.

Makes 16 oz.

HAPPY HALVAH

Tahini, the main ingredient of halvah, is high in calcium and B vitamins, good for healthy bones, hair, skin, and nails; and the raw honey helps restore digestive health. Admittedly, I used to eat halvah by the spoonful, but it also makes a great spread on apples, pears, and peaches. Add cinnamon, raw cacao, or curry spices as desired to change the flavor.

½ cup raw tahini

½ cup raw honey

1 dash Himalayan salt

Cinnamon as desired (optional)

Combine ingredients in a small bowl and whisk together until a thick paste forms. This mixture will save for up to a week in the refrigerator.

Makes 2 servings.

GORGEOUS GREEK SALAD

This is a nutrient-dense salad, and the ingredients are plentiful in most areas year-round. The spinach is a source of protein, the avocado provides an essential fatty acid, and the dressing combines to create a very balancing alkaline effect in the body. Therefore, this delicious salad is a great kitchen staple any time of the year. A basic menu item in our home, it's fun and quick to prepare.

2 cups baby spinach or red chard

1 Reed or Hass avocado

Juice of 1 lemon

¼ cup **Sweet and Red Onions**

6 grape tomatoes

1 Persian cucumber, diced or thinly
   sliced over a mandoline

2 Tbsp. extra-virgin olive oil

1 tsp. sea salt

1 tsp. cayenne pepper

Dried fruits, raw ruts or seeds,
   and dulse (optional)

Begin by slicing avocado in half lengthwise. Remove pit, scoop out the soft flesh inside, and dice. In a large mixing bowl, combine with all other ingredients. The combination of this salad's ingredients forms its "dressing," so toss them all very well so that the avocado oil gently coats the greens. Serve on a plate or in a bowl.

Makes 4 appetizer portions.

MARINATED-KALE DELI SALAD

Kale leaves provide a unique spectrum of vitamins and minerals. Kale is actually in the cabbage family, and each nutrient-dense bite is full of essential protein. This recipe is an easy preparation that, if done correctly, will become a staple for you and your family, providing quick energy and sustained health. (I recommend using black Tuscan kale, also known as dinosaur or lacinato kale, in this recipe, as it tastes the sweetest, offering an easy introduction to dark, leafy greens. However, green, purple, and white kale all make for a great salad alone or in combination.)

I head Tuscan (lacinato) kale

½ cup kalamata olives

I Reed or Hass avocado

I cup julienned cucumber

½ cup walnut pieces

Dulse, flaxseed oil, or seasoning blend such as Herbamare or our 118 all-seasoning blend (available at the restaurant and online at: **www.118degrees.com**) (optional)

Begin by slicing avocado in half lengthwise. Remove pit, scoop out the soft flesh inside, and dice. In a large mixing bowl, combine with all other salad ingredients (except kale).

De-stem the kale by pulling alongside the main stem. Layer piece over piece on a cutting board and roll tightly; then chiffonade into thin strips ¼ inch in thickness. Toss vigorously with other ingredients, massaging the oils of the avocado into the kale so that it becomes soft. This technique creates a texture that is gentler to the palate and more universally enjoyed.

Makes 4 tapas-size salads.

KALE

Kale, a descendant of cabbage, is a dark, leafy green that provides protein, calcium, antioxidants, and anti-inflammatory agents. I recommend enjoying it at least three times weekly. The minerals in this vegetable are powerfully rejuvenating—they are, in fact, the reason why kale tops the charts on many nutrient-density calculators, meaning that every bite brings you closer to optimal health. The structural properties of kale have been shown to fight many kinds of cancer, and the sterols in this particular family of plants promote strong bones and connective tissues.

Kale comes in several varieties, such as black Tuscan kale (also called lacinato or dinosaur kale), discovered in Tuscany in the late 1800s; purple curly kale, an heirloom variety; green-leaf kale; and dwarf blue kale. This known superfood is easily integrated into salads and sandwiches, and blends into smoothies to add mineral content and needed proteins.

SUPERFOOD SMOOTHIE

This smoothie was a lifesaver for me during my pregnancy, and is great for the busy weeks when it seems there isn't adequate time to prepare large meals. This recipe offers optimal nutrition as a meal-replacement shake and delivers a high-energy kick start to the day.

1 banana

1 Tbsp. almond butter or flaxseed oil

1 cup raw almond or other raw milk

1 cup fresh berries or kale

2 Tbsp. green superfood*

2 Tbsp. maca-root powder

1 Tbsp. raw cacao (optional)

1 tsp. cinnamon

Ice as desired

Blend all ingredients well and enjoy right away. Ice is optional; there has been much research to suggest that enjoying beverages at room temperature is optimal for the body's absorption of the liquid.

Makes 16 oz.

*The green superfood of your choice. I use Dr. Schulze's SuperFood Plus at the restaurant and at home because it is a blend of aquatic and land grasses, providing a full spectrum of minerals and vitamins. Chlorella, spirulina, Vitamineral Green, wheatgrass powder, and E₃Live are all excellent sources of concentrated greens.

"The beginning is
the most important
part of the work."
— PLATO

Start the Day Off Right with Nutritious, Basic Breakfasts

One of the easiest ways to begin adding more fresh, living foods into your diet is to start the day off right with a great raw breakfast. By doing so, you're already more than 30 percent raw for the day. You'll feel more clarity in the morning and really jump-start your cells. Once your body is programmed in this way early on, you'll find that it's easier to eat right all day long!

Here are some great recipes to get you going. Each dish comes complete with plant-based proteins, powerful antioxidants, and essential vitamins and minerals.

SMOOTHIE BASICS 1, 2, 3

A raw smoothie is an easy way to incorporate more living foods in your diet. Follow these simple steps for a quick, easy breakfast:

1. **Select 1–2 cups of fresh fruit in season**: Banana, berries, pineapple, and mango are all great smoothie options.

2. **Choose a liquid**: You can use either distilled water, coconut water, nut milk, or fruit juice.

3. **Supersize the energy and nutrient density:** Add a superfood of choice and any desired raw sweetener, like agave nectar or honey.

Some delicious smoothie combinations include:

- **Pomegranate Passion:** 1 banana, ¼ cup pomegranate seeds, ½ cup fresh juice of choice, 2 Tbsp. maca-root powder, and 1 Tbsp. raw honey

- **Chocolate Mint Surprise:** 1 banana or avocado, 2 Tbsp. raw cacao, 2 Tbsp. green superfood of choice, 1 cup **Hemp Milk,** 2 Tbsp. mint leaves, and 1 Tbsp. raw honey

- **Global Green:** ½ cup fresh berries, 1 banana, 2 kale leaves, 1 cup apple juice, 1 Tbsp. green superfood of choice, and 1 tsp. raw honey

- **Morning Glory:** 1 banana, 1 Tbsp. flaxseed oil, ½ cup berries, ½ cup spinach, 1 Tbsp. maca-root powder, 1 Tbsp. chia seeds, ½ cup apple juice, and 1 tsp. raw honey

All recipes yield one 16 oz. smoothie.

DAILY 5 SMOOTHIE

Five basic ingredients that can boost your health every day! This smoothie contains nutrient-dense superfoods, alkaline-forming nuts and seeds, and a selection of organic fruits and vegetables. The flaxseed oil gives your brain a jump start with essential fatty acids for the day, and the greens and nut milk are an excellent source of protein. Adding a green superfood complex provides a full chain of amino acids, and in combination with maca, will give you some great natural energy. This is a terrific smoothie for those looking to eliminate caffeine from their daily diet. Although you may make substitutions to suit your own taste and seasonal availability, you'll want to preserve the same base in order to ensure the nutritional value.

1 cup almond milk or **Hemp Milk**

1 banana or avocado

½ cup seasonal fruit, such as berries or peaches

½ cup kale or spinach

1 Tbsp. flaxseed oil or other superfoods of choice (my favorites include 1 Tbsp. supergreens powder, 1 Tbsp. maca-root powder, and 1 Tbsp. raw honey or agave nectar) (optional)

Blend all ingredients well in a high-powered blender; add 1 cup ice if desired.

Makes 16–20 oz., depending on fruit and ice.

SUPERFOOD GUIDE

— **Greens.** Green superfoods are common within living-foods diets because of the vital minerals inherent in the dark greens from both land and sea. They're also a quick and easy way to ensure proper protein intake.

- **Spirulina:** This aquatic plant is 60 percent protein and contains phytonutrients such as beta-carotene, chlorophyll, and GLA (an essential fatty acid), as well as vitamin B_{12} and iron.

- **E_3Live:** This dietary supplement contains 3–5 times more chlorophyll than wheatgrass, along with vitamin B_{12}, omega-3s, and 22 amino acids, which promote healthy digestion.

- **Superfood complexes:** Green superfoods are high in protein, chlorophyll, and essential minerals. Shop for complexes that contain aquatic and land grasses. Proteins and amino acids in combination are the building blocks of the human body, which is why these supplements are so effective for boosting nutrition quickly.

— **Essential fatty acids (EFAs), proteins, and amino acids.** Healthy hair, skin, nails, connective tissue, and musculature all start with essential fats, proteins, and amino acids.

- **Maca-root powder:** Maca-root powder contains more than 55 phytochemicals, known to elevate mood and improve endurance and blood circulation. It is also high in amino acids and B vitamins, including B_{12}.

- **Hemp:** Hemp supplements are rich in omega-3, omega-6, omega-9, and essential amino acids; are known for muscle-building ability; and are high in antioxidants to fight off disease-causing free radicals in the bloodstream.

- **Bee pollen, propolis, or royal jelly:** Bee by-products receive high antioxidant scores; they are energy enhancing and dense with nutrients, including omega-3s and B-complex vitamins.

- **Chia seeds:** These seeds are high-energy endurance superfoods, full of calcium. They slow down the conversion of carbohydrates into sugar and prolong hydration throughout the day.

- **Flaxseed:** Flax offers a superior source of protein; and it's exceptionally high in omega-3, omega-6, and omega-9.

— **Minerals and vitamins.** The following superfoods are high in minerals and vitamins to help keep blood plasma clean and aid in optimal organ function, especially the brain's.

- **Raw cacao:** Raw cacao contains mood-enhancing agents, sulfur, magnesium, and trace minerals.

- **Goji berries:** Goji berries are extremely high in antioxidants, contain 18 amino acids and vitamin C, and are 13 percent protein. They also provide calcium; magnesium; and vitamins E, B_1, B_2, and B_6.

- **Carob:** Carob is 80 percent protein and contains calcium; vitamins A, B_1, B_2, B_3, and D; potassium; magnesium; iron; and the trace mineral phosphorous.

SMOTHERED BANANA

A hearty breakfast is needed when your day is jam-packed with activities. For my smothered bananas, I prefer to use almond butter, but any nut butter works just as well. I like to add chocolate to mine, so be sure to include whatever ingredients *you* love. This is a hearty breakfast that will give you sustained energy.

1 banana

4 Tbsp. raw nut butter

1 cup **Apple-Pistachio Granola** (see next page)

1 dash cinnamon

Raw honey or agave nectar to sweeten (optional)

Slice banana lengthwise and spread nut butter of choice over surface. Sprinkle with granola and a dash of cinnamon, and drizzle with raw honey or agave.

Makes 1 serving.

APPLE-PISTACHIO GRANOLA

A 118 favorite, this granola can be enjoyed any time of the day, but is especially nice for breakfast, as it is very high in protein. (A cup of sprouted buckwheat provides more than 14 grams of usable protein.) This granola also stores very well and can be kept in your pantry in an airtight container for months. This crunchy snack is fantastic on coconut yogurt, sprinkled in smoothies, or on top of a banana smothered in almond butter. It also pairs nicely with some almond milk. Yum!

4 cups sprouted buckwheat (for sprouting instructions, see sidebar in Chapter 7)

½ cup raw agave nectar or honey

1 cup diced apples

½ cup pistachios (soaked 4 hours)

1 Tbsp. cinnamon

1 tsp. nutmeg

1 dash Himalayan salt or sea salt

Combine all ingredients in a large bowl and toss well, making sure the honey or agave and spices coat the ingredients thoroughly.

Prepare a dehydrator tray by lining with a Teflex sheet, a silicone sheet, or parchment paper to catch the liquids. Gently lay out mixture ½ inch in thickness or less. Place in dehydrator set at 118° for 12 hours. I recommend tossing the mixture about halfway through to make sure the groats dry evenly. (Wet spots may lead to fermentation.) Once the mixture is dry all the way, you'll be able to store this granola indefinitely.

Makes about 4 cups.

BREAKFAST BURRITOS

Being a Southern California native, I grew up on breakfast burritos, and although this recipe is decidedly different, I love it just the same. This is a Sunday favorite in our home that never fails to please. It is also a high-protein selection with a full spectrum of vitamins and nutrients.

For the burritos:

4 **Easy Tortillas**

½ cup **Simplicity Guacamole**

½ cup **Tomatillo Salsa**

For the filling:

1 cup shredded carrots

1 cup chopped spinach

1 large avocado, diced

1 cup chopped cremini mushrooms

1 cup thinly sliced zucchini

¼ cup chopped green onions

1½ cups **Smoky Ranchero Sauce**

Toss all filling ingredients in a large mixing bowl until well combined. Lay out tortillas on a cutting board and line the centers with the filling, evenly divided. Roll tortillas tightly around filling and top each with 2 Tbsp. salsa and 2 Tbsp. guacamole and a little extra ranchero sauce if you like yours spicy!

Makes 4 burritos.

PEACH COFFEE CAKE

Peaches are especially nice in this recipe, but if stone fruit is out of season, you may substitute berries, pears, or bananas. This dish doesn't require a dehydrator, although using one to finish it will give you a slightly different texture.

For the crust:

2 cups walnuts (pieces)

½ cup raw honey or agave nectar

1 Tbsp. cinnamon

1 tsp. nutmeg

1 tsp. vanilla paste

1 dash sea salt

For the topping:

4 large peaches

½ cup raw honey or agave nectar

¼ cup cinnamon

1 tsp. sea salt

2 shots cold-brewed espresso*

1 tsp. vanilla paste

Prepare peaches by slicing lengthwise and removing pits, leaving skins on. Cut into thin (½-inch thick or less) slices Toss into a medium-size bowl with sweetener and other topping ingredients. Toss mixture until well combined.

Place walnuts, cinnamon, nutmeg, vanilla, and sea salt in food processor and pulse until coarse, flourlike mixture forms. Switch to the processing setting and add sweetener as the mixture is turning. Stop the processor once dough ball begins to form. Press mixture into an 8-inch square glass baking dish to create crust along the bottom. Top with peach mixture. Let set for ½ hour in refrigerator if not dehydrating. If dehydrating, do so on high for 2 hours only—if using a standard dehydrator, the interior temperature will not warm past 118° in the first 2 hours of drying time.

Makes sixteen 2" × 2" pieces.

*To cold-brew espresso, simply grind the espresso bean to a fine texture and soak in purified water for 4–6 hours.

CHOCOLATE GO-GO BALLS

For eating on the run, these go-go balls are great, and the best part is that you'll feel like you're having dessert for breakfast. Raw cacao is high in magnesium and stimulates the creativity center of the brain, so these aid in concentration all day long.

2 cups raw pecans (pieces)

½ cup raw agave nectar or honey

1½ cups raw cacao

1 tsp. cinnamon

1 Tbsp. raw coconut butter (optional)

2 Tbsp. maca-root powder

2 Tbsp. supergreens powder

1 tsp. sea salt

Coconut shreds for topping

Place raw pecan pieces in a food processor with S-blade attachment. Pulse until a coarse, flourlike mixture forms. Add the cacao, cinnamon, supergreens powder, and salt. Continue pulsing until well combined. Switch to the processing setting and slowly pour in coconut butter and then sweetener. Aim for the center of the processor, and stop as soon as a dough ball begins to form. Overprocessing will result in an excess of oil in the mixture, so this is to be avoided. Scoop out onto parchment paper lined in coconut shreds and roll mixture until ball forms. If needed, freeze mixture for 15 minutes so that balls hold their shape well.

Makes twelve 2-inch balls, which will last indefinitely stored in your pantry in an airtight container.

YOUNG THAI COCONUTS

Young Thai coconuts, or "nature's hydrating elixir," are truly a miraculous treat from Mother Nature. In island communities, coconut water has been used in transfusions when blood was unavailable, as it resembles blood plasma on a cellular level. It is a natural isotonic beverage, providing a level of electrolytic balance close to that of our bodies. Coconut water can be easily absorbed into the bloodstream and can hydrate cells instantly. The flesh is high in essential fatty acids, and the oil contains many anti-inflammatory agents and has natural antifungal properties that ward off parasites.

The coconut is actually a seed, the largest we know of, and takes about a year to mature on the tree. Young Thai coconuts are harvested and used immediately, yielding a higher level of natural enzyme activity, as well as sweet water that is full of potassium. The flesh remains soft and is an excellent gourmet ingredient to create yogurts and other delectable dishes.

The most common thing I hear when people buy their first young Thai coconut is: "How do I get in there?" I've never seen a staff person or customer injure him- or herself while opening a coconut (knock on wood), and over the past ten years we've opened more than 1,000 cases together. Here is a quick guide to coconut opening:

Position the coconut on a cutting board and place the hand that will not be holding the knife on the side of the coconut to position it and hold it steady, making sure to keep your fingers clear of the top. Using a cleaver or chef's knife, aim to create a square "lid" on the top of the coconut. Press straight down, letting the weight of the knife do most of the work. Rotate the coconut a quarter turn and repeat, making a right angle with the previous cut. Repeat until you hear the interior husk crack; then you can insert your knife to lift up the top of the coconut. Don't be concerned if it takes you more than four cuts; just keep working your way around until the husk cracks.

This is a practice-makes-perfect skill, so be sure to keep trying—it only gets easier. Once the coconut is open, the water can be stored 2–4 days in the refrigerator, and the flesh for up to 7 days. Freezing the flesh is not recommended, but the coconut water makes for fun ice cubes (see the **Lemon-Mint Ice Cubes** recipe in Chapter 9)!

BERRIES-'N'-COCONUT YOGURT

Coconut yogurt is easily digested and is a nice breakfast dish for the whole family. You may choose to ferment your yogurt* if you would like to add to the health benefits of this delicious recipe.

For the yogurt:

4 cups young Thai coconut flesh

¼ cup raw honey

¼ cup coconut water

I tsp. sea salt

¼ cup lemon juice

I Tbsp. powdered acidophilus
(optional)

For the dish:

I cup fresh berries

½ cup **Berry Puree** as garnish

To prepare the yogurt, combine all ingredients in a high-powered blender. Blend until a nice thick consistency is achieved. Chill prior to serving.

In serving dishes, combine I cup coconut yogurt, followed by ¼ cup Berry Puree, and top with ½ cup fresh berries. (Serve layered in martini glasses or espresso cups for a fun presentation.)

Makes 2 servings.

*About fermenting: This yogurt can be saved up to 5 days in the refrigerator, but it will last up to 12 days if you choose to ferment. If you do add acidophilus, the taste will become stronger as it ferments. Be sure to store in the refrigerator during that time. Fermenting your yogurt aids in digestion and has been shown to assist many with strengthening the immune system.

BREAKFAST BLISS BARS

These bars can be made in advance and stored for up to a week in the refrigerator. They are topped with delicious cherries or figs, depending on the season.

2 cups macadamia nuts or walnuts

¾ cup raw honey or agave nectar

I Tbsp. raw coconut butter or shreds

2 cups cherries or dried cranberries

I Tbsp. cinnamon

I Tbsp. maca-root powder

I tsp. dried ginger root

I tsp. sea salt

In a food processor, process nuts down to a meal and add in cinnamon, maca, ginger, and sea salt. Pulse until well combined. Add in coconut butter or shreds and I¼ cups cherries or cranberries. Process to a thick paste and add in ½ cup desired sweetener from the top while processing. Continue processing until dough ball forms.

In a small bowl, combine remaining fruit and sweetener. Then press out dough mixture in a medium-size glass container, top with fruit mixture, and refrigerate for 2 hours. Remove from refrigerator and cut into desired shapes. Enjoy all week long!

Makes twelve 3" × 3" squares.

CINNAMON-WALNUT CAKES

These savory cakes are easy to take on the run, and they make a beautiful display on the countertop. The figs used in this dish are lower in sugar than other sweeteners, and high in magnesium.

4 cups raw walnuts

1 cup dried mission figs (soaked to rehydrate)

1 cup diced apples or pears

½ cup raw honey

2 Tbsp. cinnamon

1 tsp. nutmeg

½ tsp. vanilla

½ tsp. cloves

1 tsp. sea salt

In a food processor, combine the walnuts, cinnamon, vanilla, salt, nutmeg, and cloves until a light meal forms. Add in the apples or pears and the figs. Pulse the mixture until moderately combined with nuts. Switch to the processing setting and add the honey from the top, processing until dough ball forms. Scoop out mixture into 3-inch balls, 4 by 4 (16 total), on a lined dehydrator tray. Press into round, tall cakes and dehydrate at 118° for 8 hours. (If you don't have a dehydrator, you can line a glass container with parchment and follow the same protocol, refrigerating until enjoyed.) Remove from dehydrator, and keep on the countertop or in the refrigerator for enjoyment all week.

Makes 16 cakes.

"Motivation is what gets you started, habit is what keeps you going."

— ATTRIBUTED TO JIM ROHN

RAW STAPLES:
FAST RECIPES TO
BOOST YOUR HEALTH

This is a collection of recipes that are as easy as 1, 2, 3! They can quickly have you eating raw every day, enjoying fresh flavors and seasonal specialties alike!

Raw Basics is about helping people connect the dots on the road to excellent nutrition. This food is functional; nothing is added that doesn't benefit the body in some fashion. These recipes pave the way for an easy shift to a more holistic diet, one that is good for you and the planet.

I recommend that you select one day a week for preparing fresh sauces, as many keep five to seven days in the refrigerator. Eating for longevity means that fresh fruits and vegetables make up 80 percent of your diet. These basic sauces and spreads pair with lettuce cups, wraps, and stuffed vegetables to create fast and easy options.

Wraps, crackers, and breads take a while to dehydrate, so creating the basic separates in advance will decrease your preparation time. Having raw staples around that can act as quick go-to snacks for you and your friends and family is key to enjoying a life full of vibrant living foods.

BASIC SAUCES AND SPREADS

There are five categories of sauces and spreads in living-foods preparations:

1. **Vegetable purees** are just what they sound like: pureed vegetables. To create a nice creamy texture, it's essential to add an oil to emulsify the blend.

2. **Seed cheeses** are typically rich in flavor and usually have substantial body, like a hummus or pâté.

3. **Nut cheeses** are rich and smooth and contain some amount of water content to create a creamy sauce of sprouted nuts and herbs.

4. **Oil-based sauces** include dressings and pestos, ideal for coating vegetables and creating different textures in the dehydrator.

5. **Chutneys** or **tapenades,** also referred to as relishes, are blends of finely chopped savory and sweet ingredients.

A great sauce has the ability to totally transform an experience with fresh, living foods by complementing the natural flavors in vegetables.

TAHINI SPREAD

Tahini, or sesame-seed paste, creates great body in sauces and is such a functional ingredient. Recommended as part of a daily diet, it's widely used in Middle Eastern cultures as a base ingredient.

1 cup tahini

2 Roma tomatoes

1 red bell pepper

½ clove garlic

2 Tbsp. lemon juice

1 green onion

½ cup diced dill pickles

2 Tbsp. fresh dill

1 tsp. sea salt

In a blender, combine the tomatoes, red bell pepper, lemon juice, salt, garlic, and onion. Blend well into a liquid. Add in tahini and continue blending until a thick paste forms. Transfer to another container for storage, and hand-fold in dill pickles and fresh dill.

Makes 2 cups.

RED BELL PEPPER AND OLIVE TAPENADE

This tapenade is a great addition to any Italian or fusion dish. With essential fatty acids and a strong flavor profile, it provides a tasty treat for your body and mind.

2 cups kalamata olives, pitted

2 cups thinly sliced red bell peppers

½ cup fresh basil

2 cloves garlic

¼ cup extra-virgin olive oil

1 tsp. sea salt

In a food processor, combine red bell peppers, basil, garlic, olive oil, and sea salt; then pulse to a very fine diced mixture. Add in the olives and pulse to desired thickness. You may elect to create more of a paste or more of a relish depending on desired use. This mixture will store for up to 7 days in the refrigerator. If red bell peppers aren't in season, soaked sun-dried tomatoes also provide a nice base for this tapenade.

Makes 3 cups.

SIMPLICITY GUACAMOLE

Delicious any time of the year, guacamole is a standby treat for any Mexican dish, or on your favorite vegetables or crackers. The oils from the avocado are especially nourishing for the hair and skin, great to get you "into the glow"!

2 large Hass avocados

¼ cup lemon juice

1 Tbsp. sea salt

1 tsp. white pepper (optional)

Cut the avocados lengthwise and remove pits. Gently scoop out the soft flesh inside and place in a medium-size mixing bowl. Using a fork, press down and combine avocados, lemon, sea salt, and pepper if desired. Repeat motion until desired texture is achieved. Alternatively, you can use a handheld immersion blender to make a rich, creamy guacamole by pressing blender down into the bowl repeatedly. Enjoy within the same day for optimal taste and nutrition.

Makes 1½ cups.

SUN-DRIED TOMATO KETCHUP

Sun-dried tomatoes have a strong flavor profile, as well as an easy texture to create ketchup with. This blend can actually be stored in the refrigerator for up to 14 days and be made year-round utilizing locally dried tomatoes.

2 cups sun-dried tomatoes

¼ cup extra-virgin olive oil

¼ cup raw honey

1 tsp. sea salt

2 Tbsp. lemon juice

In a blender, combine olive oil, honey, salt, and lemon juice. Blend until well combined; then add in the sun-dried tomatoes and continue blending until a thick paste forms. Store in the refrigerator.

Makes 1½ cups.

SMOKY RANCHERO SAUCE

Growing up in Southern California, I was greatly influenced by the Mexican culture just over the border. This recipe is a family favorite that can be combined with the Whipped Avocado Spread and Tomatillo Salsa (on the following pages) to make a colorful and delicious trio.

2 cups macadamia nuts

1½ cups young Thai coconut water

1 Roma tomato

2 chipotle peppers

2 Tbsp. dried basil

2 Tbsp. chili powder

2 Tbsp. raw honey or agave nectar

2 Tbsp. extra-virgin olive oil

¼ cup lemon juice

1 tsp. sea salt

In a high-powered blender, combine all ingredients except macadamia nuts. Blend until well combined. Add in the nuts and blend to a thick puree. This sauce keeps for up to 7 days in the refrigerator.

Makes 4 cups.

WHIPPED AVOCADO SPREAD

We use this recipe as a butter replacement in our family, and it also makes a nice creamy nut-free spread to enjoy on pretty much everything. It's simple and can even be whisked by hand if you're removed from electricity.

2 Reed or Hass avocados
1 lime
1 clove garlic
1 tsp. Himalayan or sea salt
1 tsp. raw honey or agave nectar

Begin by slicing avocados in half lengthwise. Remove pits, scoop out the soft flesh inside, and place in an oversize bowl (big enough to have space to really blend ingredients). Cut lime in half and press out the juice into the bowl, watching for seeds, and then add all remaining ingredients. With a handheld immersion blender, whip to form a rich, creamy consistency with no lumpy pieces. The avocados won't brown due to the lime juice, so this spread will keep for up to 4 days.

Makes roughly 1 cup.

TOMATILLO SALSA

Tomatillos are such a vibrant part of any dish. For starters, they're green! They have a nice tart flavor and are delicious when combined with jalapeños or serrano chilies. (To prepare the tomatillo, gently remove the husk and rinse.)

4 cups diced tomatillos

1 cup chopped green onions

2 Tbsp. diced garlic cloves

½ cup lemon juice

2 serrano or jalapeño peppers, finely chopped

1 tsp. sea salt

For this recipe, it helps if much of the dicing is done in advance so that very little processing must take place in a machine. This recipe can actually be done pico de gallo–style completely by hand if necessary. After all ingredients are well chopped, combine in a food processor and pulse to desired consistency. I like mine with nice body, but you may enjoy more of a liquid. This salsa keeps for up to 5 days.

Makes 2½ cups (medium body).

Pesto Aioli

This is a blend of oil-based and nut cream sauces. It is an excellent replacement for mayonnaise and is an easy go-to dip for all kinds of crudités.

2 cups fresh basil
1 cup extra-virgin olive oil
1 cup pistachios
4 cloves garlic
1 tsp. sea salt
½ cup young Thai coconut water

In a blender, combine ½ cup olive oil, coconut water, and pistachios. Blend well and set aside. Then blend the basil, remaining olive oil, garlic, and salt to create an emulsion. Add the milky pistachio mixture while the blender is on. Refrigerate, and use within 10 days.

Makes 2½ cups.

PUMPKIN-SEED CHEESE

Pumpkin seeds are an excellent cancer-prevention food and make a delicious cheese that is fast and easy to prepare.

2 cups pumpkin seeds
   (soaked 4 hours)

1 Roma tomato

2 cloves garlic

1 chipotle pepper (optional)

1 green onion

Juice of 1 lemon

1 tsp. sea salt

2 Tbsp. chili powder

In a food processor with S-blade attachment in place, load seeds and process down to a paste. Add all other ingredients and continue processing until well combined. This cheese keeps for up to 7 days in the refrigerator.

Makes 2 cups.

Raw Parmesan Cheese

Sprinkle your next salad or entrée with a delicious, flavorful topping that also adds essential fatty acids and functional proteins to your meal. This is a great recipe to make in bulk and keep in your cupboard for all-the-time use and is wonderful to take on the go.

2 cups macadamia nuts

2 Roma tomatoes

½ cup lemon juice

2 Tbsp. nutritional yeast

1 tsp. sea salt

1 cup water

Blend all ingredients in a high-powered blender until well combined. Spread mixture over a covered dehydrator tray (¼ inch in thickness). Dehydrate for 12 hours until cheese can be crumbled apart gently. Store in an airtight container in the pantry indefinitely.

Makes ½ cup.

COCONUT-CURRY SAUCE

This is an Indian-style curry sauce that is fairly mild in flavor. You can easily spice it up by blending in one or two Thai peppers.

I cup macadamia nuts

I Tbsp. raw coconut butter or young Thai coconut flesh

I date

I clove garlic

4 Tbsp. yellow curry powder

2 Tbsp. chopped sweet onion

2 cups coconut water

Blend all ingredients except macadamia nuts in a high-powered blender until well combined. Add in the nuts and blend to a thick sauce. This curry saves 7–10 days in the refrigerator.

Makes 4 cups.

HEIRLOOM VARIETIES

Heirloom seeds haven't been cross-pollinated or hybridized to create a stronger crop and are the descendants of what was found growing naturally during early civilization. Heirloom varieties are thus more susceptible to pests and growing conditions, but the fruits and vegetables they yield also have a higher density of minerals and vitamins—by at least 30 percent.

Heirloom varieties are often characterized by fun and different shapes and colors, unlike the uniform appearance of some of the fruits and vegetables we've grown used to seeing with modern farming. Heirloom tomatoes, for example, come in several varieties, such as Brandywine, green zebra, and sweet yellow.

HEIRLOOM-TOMATO BRUSCHETTA

Heirloom tomatoes make a festive treat; their natural flavor is so intense that you barely have to add anything to create a gourmet masterpiece.

2 heirloom tomatoes

1 cup fresh chopped basil

2 cloves garlic

6 Tbsp. extra-virgin olive oil

1 tsp. raw honey

1 tsp. Himalayan sea salt

Dice the heirloom tomatoes, discarding the stem, and place the pieces in a mixing bowl. Add in the remaining ingredients and toss well. Serve on avocado rounds or **Sprouted-Chia Bread.**

Makes 4 cups.

Roma-Tomato Marinara

Marinara sauce is a great basic staple for all of your Italian dishes. It's a quick and easy preparation and highlights some delicious flavors, especially basil and garlic.

6 Roma tomatoes

½ cup fresh basil

2 cloves garlic

¼ cup extra-virgin olive oil

1 tsp. sea salt

1 tsp. raw agave nectar (optional)

Combine all ingredients except olive oil in a high-powered blender. Blend until a thick puree forms. Then slowly add the oil to the mixture while blending to emulsify the sauce. Refrigerate, and use within 4 days.

Makes 2 cups.

BASIC RED SPICE SAUCE

This is a great condiment for Latin dishes, as well as a perfect garnish on simple vegetables and crudités platters. Although basic in nature, the flavor is intense and combines well with several other nut- and seed-based sauces.

2 Roma tomatoes

1 red bell pepper

1 chipotle pepper

¼ cup extra-virgin olive oil

1 tsp. sea salt

1 tsp. chili powder

Combine all ingredients in a high-powered blender. Blend until a thick puree forms. Refrigerate, and use within 4 days of preparation.

Makes 1 cup.

"At first people refuse to believe that a strange new thing can be done, then they begin to hope it can be done, then they see it can be done— then it is done and all the world wonders why it was not done centuries ago."

— FRANCES HODGSON BURNETT

Simple Salads
for Everyday
Enjoyment

Simplicity is the key when starting out so that your time in the kitchen doesn't feel overwhelming. The living-foods lifestyle dictates that you prepare many of your own fresh foods and eat out less often. Many of these salad recipes can be enjoyed over a three- to five-day period. They're all quick and easy, and high in nutrient density from fresh, living fruits and vegetables. These vibrant dishes are great for eating on the go and work as healthful treats just about any time of the day.

MARINATED-SHIITAKE SALAD WITH TRUFFLE DRESSING

Shiitake mushrooms are used in traditional Asian medicine to support immune function and contain a fair amount of protein. Their raw flavor is a bonus in recipes because it has such a strong savory note, with an earthy taste. The vegetable combination in this salad spans the rainbow and packs a flavorful punch of vitamins.

For the salad:

1 goldbar or crookneck squash

1 zucchini

8 large shiitake mushrooms

2 stalks of green onion

1 red bell pepper

1 piece of red chard

For the dressing:

1 Tbsp. miso

½ cup extra-virgin olive oil

¼ cup lemon juice or coconut aminos

1 tsp. truffle oil

1 small clove garlic

Blend all dressing ingredients well and set aside. (In order to keep the mixture as a nice liquid that is easy to toss with the salad ingredients, don't store in the refrigerator.)

Julienne the squash and zucchini on a mandoline. Clean mushrooms well, remove stems, and slice lengthwise in ¼-inch-thick strips. Marinate mushrooms and squash in ¼ cup dressing while preparing the other vegetables. Chiffonade the green onions, and cut the red bell pepper into ¼-inch-thick slices (after removing the stem and seeds). Roll the chard, and chiffonade into fine pieces. Combine all vegetables in a bowl. Toss well and coat with an additional 4–6 Tbsp. dressing.

Makes 4 appetizer or 2 entrée servings.

CALIFORNIA COBB SALAD
WITH GREEN GODDESS DRESSING

In California, many fresh fruits and vegetables are enjoyed year-round. This salad is a collage of flavor and vibrant color.

For the salad:

2 ears white or yellow corn

2 Hass avocados, diced

1 carrot, shredded

2 green onions, finely chopped

1 cucumber, diced

4 cups mixed baby greens

For the dressing:

1 cup tahini

2 Roma tomatoes

1 red bell pepper

1 clove garlic

1 tsp. sea salt

1 Tbsp. dried basil

1 Tbsp. dried rosemary

¼ cup lemon juice

In a blender, combine all dressing ingredients and blend into a nice creamy consistency.

Place greens in a medium-size bowl for tossing. Lay the corn flat on a cutting board and cut from the cob, rotating until all the kernels are removed, and add this to the greens. Add half of the diced avocado, along with the carrots, green onions, and cucumber. Then mix in 4 Tbsp. dressing and toss all together.

In a separate bowl, place the remaining avocado and another 4 Tbsp. dressing. Toss well. Layer each salad using a compression mold, with first ¼ cup avocado mixture, then ½ cup salad, then ¼ cup avocado mixture, and another ½ cup salad. Compress, and turn out onto a plate. Drizzle with additional dressing as desired.

Makes 4 tapas-size salads.

MANDARIN-ORANGE SALAD
WITH SWEET MISO DRESSING

This Asian-inspired salad is a delicious, crisp option in the late winter or early spring. The flavor of the mandarin orange and the creamy texture of the avocado and pecans make for a nice contrast.

For the salad:

4 cups mixed baby greens

1 cup peeled fresh mandarin oranges or tangerines

1 cup pecan pieces

1 cup diced avocado

1 cup micro-greens

For the dressing:

1 cup extra-virgin olive oil

¼ cup lemon juice

¼ cup orange juice

1 clove garlic

1 Tbsp. agave nectar

1 tsp. miso paste

1 green onion

1 tsp. sea salt

Blend all dressing ingredients in a high-powered blender until well emulsified. The mixture should look rich and creamy. Refrigerate for up to 10 days. (Makes 1½ cups.)

Slice the mandarin oranges or tangerines and toss with ¼ cup dressing until well coated. Then add in pecan pieces and toss. Finally, add in baby greens and toss again until the salad mixture is well combined. Plate, and garnish with avocado and micro-greens.

Makes 2 medium-size portions.

CHARD-ROLL SALAD

Chard comes in a variety of colors, denoting different vitamin and mineral compositions. This is a hearty green that tastes sweet and makes a very nice wrap. This leaf-wrapped recipe is a delicious treat that can be enjoyed almost year-round.

4 large chard leaves

6 cups baby spinach

2 cups fresh or dried mission figs, evenly sliced (if using dried figs, soak first to rehydrate)

½ cup thinly sliced red bell peppers

½ cup **Pesto Aioli**

Begin by laying chard out flat on a cutting board. Carefully remove hard stem by cutting around it; discard. Layer remaining sides of chard one on top of the other so that they overlap and form a basic wrap to hold a filling. In a medium-size bowl, toss the spinach, figs, and Pesto Aioli until well coated. On each leaf, layer red bell peppers, then 1½ cups spinach mixture. Wrap chard around mixture, tightly rolling from top to bottom, and close with a toothpick. Enjoy by picking up or cutting through with a knife and fork.

Makes 4 appetizer portions.

Heirloom Herb Salad
with Dill Dressing

Heirloom greens, such as dwarf blue kale, and fresh herbs are easy to grow in backyard planter boxes, and make for great starter salads that are full of flavor. I particularly love this recipe in the winter, as the herbs make it naturally warming to the body.

For the salad:

4 cups heirloom greens (kale, Malva, sweet greens, or red oak lettuce)

2 cups fresh herbs (basil, arugula, dill, parsley, cilantro, and green onions)

½ cup pomegranate seeds (optional)

½ cup slivered almonds

For the dressing:

1 cup extra-virgin olive oil

½ cup macadamia nuts

¼ cup lemon juice

1 clove garlic

1 tsp. sea salt

2 Tbsp. dried dill

Blend all dressing ingredients well in a high-powered blender. This dressing will keep in the refrigerator for up to 10 days. (Makes 2 cups.)

Toss all salad ingredients well after chopping the greens and herbs down to bite-size portions. Coat with ½ cup dressing and toss lightly. Layer on plate, add additional dressing as desired, and enjoy.

Makes 2 entrée-size or 4 tapas-size servings.

FARMING IN THE MODERN WORLD: WHERE DOES OUR FOOD COME FROM?

Farming in today's world has evolved from the original agricultural practices of our ancestors over the centuries; and ensuring the quality of our fruits, vegetables, seeds, nuts, and grains is now more important than ever. There are many growing techniques and new ideas that are designed to speed agriculture production in order to meet the demand of an ever-expanding population. However, studies indicate that organic and biodynamic farming produces more nutrient-dense fruits and vegetables, although the yield is smaller. How do we navigate this ever-changing industry that plays such a vital role in our everyday health? Staying up-to-date and making informed decisions is a necessary first step.

When shopping for produce, you may hear the following terms: *organic, in transition, pesticide free, conventional, non-GMO,* and *biodynamic.* Here are basic explanations of a few of these terms and what you should know in order to protect your health and that of your family:

— **Organic.** Farming organically involves committing to two principles: *ecological production practices* and *maintaining organic integrity in the final produce.* Ecological production entails using farming and ranching techniques and materials that conserve and build the soil resource; pollute little; and encourage development of a healthy, diverse agro-ecosystem, which supports natural pest management.

Prospective organic producers commit in advance that prohibited substances (synthetic fertilizers and pesticides) must not have been used on the land for three full years preceding harvest of the first organic crop. Farms or specific fields that don't yet meet this requirement may be considered *in transition.* These farms—labeled *pesticide free,* meaning that synthetic chemicals aren't being used on current crops now but have been in the recent past—are waiting for the soil to mature.

— **Biodynamic.** Biodynamic agriculture is a method of organic farming that considers a farm to be a unified and individual organism. Relying on what is locally present to maintain balance in the growing region is a key component of biodynamic farming. Basically, nothing is added or taken away. Old crops are tilled into the soil to fertilize for the next season. Herbal preparations are used as natural pest control, and lunar harvesting cycles are referred to. Plants cultivated via this method have high mineral density, oftentimes due to the fact that the land is properly rotated and the integrity of the soil stays intact.

— **Sustainable.** Sustainable growing practices and sustainable crops are those that ensure the longevity of agriculture and the ability of plants to reproduce over time, ensuring the health of the land for future generations.

The growing and harvesting environment, the planting and cultivation practices, and the treatment of the seeds and crops while in the ground all affect the food that goes onto our plates. Many seeds—primarily soy, wheat, corn, and canola—are now genetically modified to resist pests, and in terms of farming history, have only just recently been introduced. There is a striking rise in allergies associated with these specific crops. We're unsure of the effects of *GMOs* (genetically modified organisms) on human health. The best way to avoid such products is to choose organic produce wherever possible, as GMO seeds go against the principles of organic cultivation.

ROMAINE CHOPPED SALAD
WITH RANCH DRESSING

There is nothing like the fresh, crisp taste of romaine. I like to create this salad by tossing the ingredients in a bowl and then serving them over another piece of whole romaine for a nice look on the plate. Romaine grows most months of the year, so this salad is an easy weekly staple.

For the salad:

4 cups chopped romaine (with additional whole pieces for plating, if desired)

½ cup **Sweet and Red Onions**

¼ cup chopped kalamata olives

2 cups chopped tomatoes

1 cup diced cucumber

For the dressing:

1 cup extra-virgin olive oil

½ cup macadamia nuts

¼ cup water

1 tsp. raw honey

1 clove garlic

1 tsp. onion powder

2 Tbsp. dried Italian seasoning

1 tsp. pink Himalayan salt

For the dressing, combine all ingredients except lemon juice and olive oil and blend briefly to create a liquid base. Add juice and oil; and blend on high for about 30 seconds until a rich, creamy dressing forms. The dressing will keep for up to 8 days in the refrigerator. (Makes 2 cups.)

In a large bowl, vigorously toss the romaine, tomatoes, cucumber, and olives with 1 cup dressing. Scoop out onto plates (and over whole pieces of romaine, if desired), and top with marinated onions and additional dressing.

Makes 2 entrée-size or 4 tapas-size servings.

LONGEVITY SALAD
WITH LEMON DRESSING

Eat this salad every day for superior health and vitality.* This recipe is a perfect combination of vitamins and minerals, essential fatty acids, omega-3 and omega-6, iron, B vitamins, and more. The ultimate in functional foods, the ingredients will nourish you to the very core.

For the salad:

4 cups chopped dark, leafy greens (for example, kale, spinach, chard, collards, or mustard greens)

⅓ cup diced avocado

½ cup dulse pieces

I cup diced cucumber

½ cup hemp seeds

For the dressing:

2 Tbsp. flaxseed oil

Juice of I lemon

I tsp. sea salt or Herbamare seasoning blend

I dash cayenne pepper

Toss all salad ingredients well in a large mixing bowl. Make sure to pull apart the dulse pieces so that they're well mixed in and not clumped together. Drizzle with flaxseed oil and lemon juice and begin to toss again, sprinkling in seasonings to finish. Enjoy while this salad is still crisp and fresh.

Makes 2 entrée-size or 4 tapas-size servings.

*If you do enjoy this salad daily, rotate your greens in order to balance your nutrient intake.

"There's a difference between interest and commitment. When you're interested in doing something, you do it only when circumstances permit. When you're committed to something, you accept no excuses, only results."

— AUTHOR UNKNOWN

Starter Soups and Basic Marinated Vegetables

Simple soups and marinated vegetables are a nice way to add more living foods to your diet, especially in the wintertime. These are very warming and calming dishes that can easily replace your standard "comfort-food" fare.

As soon as there is an emotional tug, many of us look for something warm and soothing for nourishment, and these recipes are a great option. There is a common misconception that raw foods must all be cold. These preparations are designed to be enjoyed warm: 118° is actually pretty hot!

STARTER SOUPS

Soups are a quick and easy fix for a meal or snack, and can be used during cleansing regimens to give the digestive system a break. There are three ways to create a warm soup:

1. You can use water that is heated to 118° on the stove or in a hot-water machine.

2. You can place the soup in the dehydrator after blending, which will also bring out more of the flavors of the herbs.

3. If using a high-powered blender, you can warm the soup as you're blending it. Gently keep your hand on the side of the canister and stop the blender when it's hot to the touch.

No matter how you prepare the soup, you'll find a superior flavor if you follow the steps to emulsify it and create a nice broth.

BASIC VEGETABLE STOCK

Use this recipe as a base to prepare delicious vegetable soups. This is a core recipe; feel free to add your favorite spices to create even more zest in the final product.

Pass the following ingredients through a juicer:

9 stalks celery

2 tomatoes

2 carrots

1 cucumber

2 zucchini

Then transfer the juice to a basic blender and add the following ingredients:

¼ cup olive oil

1 tsp. sea salt

Blend well. If desired, add dried herbs and seasonings at this stage. This stock keeps 5–7 days in the refrigerator and can be blended with other fresh vegetables to create a savory seasonal soup.

Makes 16 oz.

SWEET MISO SOUP

A calming soup is always a welcome relief on a rainy day, and this recipe is especially nice for balancing immune function and aiding digestion. It can be enjoyed in combination with a meal or alone.

For the soup:

2 cups coconut water or
  Basic Vegetable Stock
  (see previous page)

2 Tbsp. miso paste

1 green onion

1 Tbsp. tahini

1 yellow or goldbar squash,
  cut in quarters

2 shiitake mushrooms (optional)

1 clove garlic

1 tsp. sea salt

For garnish:

½ cup dulse

1 Hass avocado, sliced

Vegetables of choice

In a blender, combine all soup ingredients until rich and creamy. Pour into bowls for serving and top with garnishes.

Makes 2 entrée-size or 4 appetizer servings.

GREEN CURRY SOUP

This is a nice, sweet curry soup that can easily be spiced up by adding in Thai peppers or cayenne. Try it as is, and spice to taste.

2 zucchini

1 Tbsp. miso paste

2 cups hot water

1 clove garlic

2 Tbsp. yellow curry powder

1 tsp. raw honey

1 tsp. sea salt

¼ cup extra-virgin olive oil

Blend all ingredients except olive oil in a high-powered blender. After mixture is well combined, slowly add the oil from the top while blending to emulsify, and create a nice body for the broth.

Makes 2 entrée-size or 4 appetizer servings.

FRENCH ONION SOUP

French onion soup was a childhood favorite of mine, and this flavorful version has an added immune-boosting bonus. I love to share it with family and friends in the winter. Beware: this recipe has a strong flavor, so it's not for the faint of heart (or taste buds!).

For the soup:

1 sweet onion

2 portobello mushrooms

9 stalks celery

2 zucchini

1 clove garlic

1 tsp. sea salt

1 cup hot water

¼ cup olive oil

For garnish:

½ cup **Raw Parmesan Cheese**

½ cup **Marinated Mushrooms**

Herbs of choice (try basil or cumin)

Pass the celery and zucchini through a juicer. Add the juice to a high-powered blender and combine with mushrooms, onion, garlic, salt, and hot water. Blend into a thick, frothy mixture. Once you reach this stage, slowly add the olive oil while blending to emulsify the mixture. Pour into serving bowls and top with garnish. This soup should keep up to 3 days in the refrigerator.

Makes 2 entrée-size or 4 appetizer servings.

TOMATILLO AND AVOCADO SOUP

This is a chilled soup that is quite refreshing during the summer months. It makes a great appetizer for Latin meals like the Verde Tacos (in the next chapter) or enchiladas.

For the soup:

6 tomatillos

2 cucumbers

1 jalapeño pepper

¼ cup diced onion

2 cloves garlic

¼ cup lemon juice

1 cup coconut water

¼ cup extra-virgin olive oil

1 tsp. sea salt

For garnish:

2 cups diced avocado

½ cup diced cilantro

Lime wedges

In a high-powered blender, combine all ingredients except olive oil. Blend until well combined, and then slowly add the oil from the top of the blender while it's still on to emulsify liquid. Chill soup, and when ready to serve, top with a generous amount of diced avocado and fresh cilantro. Serve with a lime wedge to squeeze on top while enjoying.

Makes 2 entrée-size or 4 appetizer servings.

MARINATED VEGETABLES

Marinating vegetables in the dehydrator or refrigerator will bring out different flavors and textures and create an ingredient with a lot of depth. Some of the marinated vegetables must be used within a couple days, but a few can be kept all week to create a flavorful garnish on many dishes.

SWEET AND RED ONIONS

These tasty treats are a delicious addition to soups, salads, and wraps, and create a nice bold flavor when added to any entrée. While in the dehydrator, the onions will produce a potent aroma throughout your house, so it's best to prepare them in advance if entertaining.

4 cups thinly sliced red and sweet
   brown onions
¼ cup extra-virgin olive oil
¼ cup raw agave nectar
I tsp. sea salt

Toss all ingredients well in a medium-size bowl. Gently massage the marinade into the fiber of the onions. Refrigerate, and let sit at least I day prior to use. For additional flavor, dehydrate at 115° for 4 hours. These onions keep for up to 10 days in the refrigerator.

Makes 3 cups.

Marinated Mushrooms

A delicious mushroom flavor combination, this recipe is a must-have in any gourmet living-foods kitchen.

2 cups diced portobello mushrooms

2 cups thinly sliced shiitake mushrooms

2 cups maitake mushrooms

1 cup extra-virgin olive oil

3 Tbsp. fresh thyme

1 tsp. sea salt

2 Tbsp. balsamic vinegar (optional)

1 Tbsp. truffle oil (optional)

2 Tbsp. raw honey (optional)

In a medium-size bowl, toss the mushrooms together, and then add in sea salt and thyme. Toss with olive oil and other optional ingredients until mushrooms are well coated, and place over covered dehydrator tray. Dehydrate at 118° for 4 hours or until desired taste and texture are achieved. The longer the mushrooms are left in the dehydrator, the softer they become as the oil expands. Refrigerate leftovers for up to 5 days. If you don't have a dehydrator, you can just refrigerate this mixture and let sit for 12 hours prior to enjoying.

Makes 4 cups.

3-VEGETABLE BLEND

This basic blend goes with a variety of dishes.

2 cups sliced yellow squash or zucchini

2 cups thinly sliced red bell peppers

2 cups diced mushrooms or eggplant

2 Roma tomatoes

½ cup extra-virgin olive oil

1 clove garlic

1 tsp. sea salt

1 Tbsp. chili powder or dried basil
(choose based on accompanying
dish)

In a blender, combine tomatoes, olive oil, garlic, sea salt, and dried herbs. Blend well until emulsified. In a large mixing bowl, pour marinade over vegetables. Toss until well coated. Place on a covered dehydrator tray and dehydrate at 118° for 4 hours. The longer the vegetables sit in the dehydrator, the softer they will become. Enjoy this mixture warm, and then store leftovers in the refrigerator for up to 2 days.

Makes 5 cups.

EGGPLANT BALSAMICO

Eggplant is a great option during winter months and provides a nice weight and texture in many Mediterranean and Italian dishes.

4 cups thinly sliced eggplant
I cup **Sweet Miso Dressing**
½ cup chopped parsley
¼ cup balsamic vinegar
I tsp. sea salt

In a large mixing bowl, toss the eggplant with the dressing, sea salt, and chopped parsley, making sure it's well coated and absorbs the dressing. Then on a covered dehydrator tray, layer the eggplant so that each round barely touches the one next to it. Dehydrate at 118° for 2–4 hours. Halfway through, drizzle balsamic vinegar over the top and allow to soak in.

Makes 3 cups.

COCONUT-CURRY VEGETABLES

These veggies are a nice addition to many dishes and can also be enjoyed alone as a flavorful snack. This recipe keeps well, so it's a good idea to make it in advance to enjoy throughout the week.

2 cups chopped cauliflower

2 cups chopped broccoli

2 cups snap peas or regular peas

1 cup **Coconut-Curry Sauce**

2 cups spinach (optional)

In a large mixing bowl, toss together all vegetables and sauce until everything is well combined. If enjoying right away, add in spinach to the mixture. Place on a covered dehydrator tray and dehydrate at 118° for 3 hours.

Makes 6 cups.

TUSCAN VEGETABLES

Tuscany is a dense growing region of Italy and the agricultural hub of the country. This blend of sweet and savory vegetables can be added to any salad or enjoyed as a side dish.

2 cups chopped Tuscan (lacinato) kale

2 cups thinly sliced tomatoes

2 cups thinly sliced Italian squash

2 cups chopped cremini mushrooms

2 Tbsp. dried basil

1 cup extra-virgin olive oil

1 tsp. sea salt

2 Tbsp. raw honey

2 Tbsp. diced garlic

In a large mixing bowl, combine vegetables, dried basil, sea salt, and garlic. Toss well. Then add the olive oil and honey, and continue tossing until all veggies are coated. Place on a covered dehydrator tray and dehydrate at 118° for up to 4 hours. Enjoy immediately. Refrigerate leftovers and use within 2 days.

Makes 6 cups.

ALMOND AND ROSEMARY GREEN BEANS

When in season, green beans are a fantastic option, with a beautiful texture and nice flavor. I recommend purchasing them farm fresh for use in this recipe.

6 cups green beans

½ cup thinly sliced red onions

½ cup slivered almonds

1 cup extra-virgin olive oil

2 Tbsp. finely chopped garlic

1 Tbsp. fresh rosemary

1 tsp. sea salt

Begin by cutting off and discarding the sides of the green beans where the stems attach; then chop beans down to 1-inch pieces. In a blender combine the olive oil, rosemary, garlic, and sea salt; blend until well combined, forming an herb infusion. In a medium-size mixing bowl, combine the green beans, almonds, and red onions. Pour in herb infusion and toss together. At this point you may refrigerate the mixture for 12 hours before use or place on a covered dehydrator tray and dehydrate at 118° for up to 4 hours.

Makes 6 cups.

"All you need is love. But a little chocolate now and then doesn't hurt."
— CHARLES M. SCHULZ

Easy Entrée Selections and Fast Desserts

Sandwiches, wraps, and desserts are easy and delicious ways to enjoy more fresh, vibrant foods. Lunch is a great time to get vital nutrition to provide fuel for the rest of your day; and living desserts, often high in protein and low on the glycemic index, make fantastic breakfasts or late-afternoon snacks.

QUICK-FIX SANDWICHES AND WRAPS

These recipes are easy once the basic breads and wraps are prepared. I suggest picking a day once a week to make these pantry items. This shortcut will decrease your time in the kitchen, as well as provide options for unplanned meals that are still very nutrient dense.

VERDE TACOS

This recipe is a tribute to the life-giving essence of greens (*verde* means "green" in Spanish), with the tantalizing flavors of tomatillo and the fresh, crisp texture of cucumber.

For the Spicy Pepitas:

2 cups soaked pepitas*

1 Tbsp. raw agave nectar or honey

1 tsp. chili powder

1 tsp. sea salt

For the tacos:

6 Tbsp. **Tomatillo Salsa**

2 ears white or yellow corn

1 cucumber (medium size)

2 cups fresh baby spinach

1 head Napa cabbage

2 cups **Pumpkin-Seed Cheese**

In advance, prepare the Spicy Pepitas by tossing all ingredients in a medium-size mixing bowl. When well coated, spread seeds over a covered dehydrator tray and dehydrate at 118° for 6–8 hours. Store indefinitely in an airtight container once fully dried to use as a garnish.

To prepare the tacos, carefully cut the corn from the cob (it's helpful to do so with the corn lying sideways on the cutting board). Combine with the baby spinach in a bowl. Dice the cucumber with the skin on and add to the mix. Remove the outer pieces of the Napa cabbage head one by one, clean, and cut off the portion of the leaves closest to the stem. Line up leaves on cutting board so that the cuplike curvature is facing up, ready to be filled. Spread Pumpkin-Seed Cheese inside each leaf and then layer with spinach mixture. Top with Tomatillo Salsa and a sprinkling of Spicy Pepitas.

Makes 4 large, or 6 appetizer, tacos (depending on size of Napa cabbage leaves used).

*Soaked for 6 hours. This isn't a requirement but will activate more of the enzyme content of the seed, making it easier to digest.

SURFER SANDWICH

This sandwich was inspired by the strength and perseverance seen up and down the coasts of the world as those who love the ocean harmonize with the waves meeting the shore. It's no surprise that surfing is a sport you must power up for, and this recipe is full of high-energy protein and healthy carbohydrates to "take on the surf," literally and metaphorically.

For the Sprouted-Chia Bread:

2 cups sprouted grain* (Kamut, rye, wheat berry, or spelt**)

¼ cup raw chia seeds

¼ cup extra-virgin olive oil

1 tsp. sea salt

¼ cup sweet onions

For the filling:

4 cups finely chopped Tuscan (lacinato) kale

2 medium Hass avocados, diced

2 cups mixed vegetables of choice

2 Tbsp. **Whipped Avocado Spread**

Attach the S blade to a food processor, and pour in the sprouted grain and sweet onions from the bread ingredients. Process this mixture until blended well. Add the salt, olive oil, and chia seeds and process further until a dough ball forms. Stop processing as soon as this occurs so as not to overheat the grains. Remove mixture. Spread out evenly (about ¼ inch in thickness) over a covered dehydrator tray, using a spatula dipped in warm water to prevent sticking. Dehydrate for 4 hours at 115°. Flip bread over and dehydrate for 1 more hour. The bread should be dry to the touch. Avoid overdrying so it doesn't become undesirably crunchy.

In a medium-size mixing bowl, combine the avocado and kale. Massage together until the kale leaves are well coated with avocado.

Cut the bread into squares and then slice in half diagonally to form triangles. Layer on Whipped Avocado Spread, and top with 1 cup kale-avocado blend and ½ cup mixed vegetables per sandwich.

Makes 2 entrée-size or 4 appetizer portions.

*To sprout the grains, they must first be soaked in water for 8 hours. They don't need to be refrigerated during this time but should be covered lightly. Rinse the grains well and allow to sprout on your countertop for about 3 days. A small tail should begin to emerge. Use grains immediately when they reach this point for best results.

**If you're gluten intolerant, try substituting almond pulp for the grains. The recipe won't yield as much bread, but it will taste fantastic.

Garden Rolls

Garden Rolls are a delight year-round and are designed to feature what is fresh and in season. This is a choose-your-own-adventure dish: try 2–3 of the freshest vegetables you can find, and begin by slicing them thin in a food processor or julienning them over a mandoline.

For the Easy Tortillas*:

2 cups ground golden flaxseed

2 cups diced squash

¼ cup raw chia seeds

½ cup sprouted Kamut (optional)

2 Tbsp. chili powder

2½ cups water

For the filling:

2 cups fresh seasonal vegetables
(*suggestion:* portobello mushrooms, bell peppers, eggplant, and onions)

2 cups fresh spinach or kale

For relish:

2 cups grape tomatoes

¼ cup dried-herb blend or chopped fresh herbs

1 Hass avocado, diced

2 Tbsp. tahini

To begin, combine all tortilla ingredients in a blender, adding the water and squash first and then the seeds and herbs. Blend well on high. Spread in ¼-inch-thick rounds on dehydrator trays covered with a silicone sheet, saran wrap, or a Teflex sheet. Dehydrate at 115° for 5 hours. (Makes 6 tortillas.)

To prepare the filling, thinly slice all vegetables and finely chop greens; set aside for later use. Then to prepare the relish, pulse the grape tomatoes and herbs in a food processor until lightly chopped together. Add the tahini and avocado, and pulse for just a moment until mixed together but not creamy.

To finish the dish, lay out dried tortillas on a cutting board. Layer each with ¼ cup relish, then ½ cup filling. Roll tortilla tightly around mixture. Let sit for a moment so that the contents have time to settle. Slice in half and serve at room temperature.

Makes 6 entrée portions.

*If you don't have time to make a tortilla, these wraps are fantastic in collard-green or red chard leaves.

TOE-TAPPIN' TOSTADITOS

Crunchy delights are among my favorite midday meals. Research suggests that eating five small meals daily is better than three large ones. These Tostaditos fit the bill perfectly! This is also a fun preparation to have on hand for afternoon snacks.

For the Tostadito Shells:

2 cups sprouted buckwheat (see next page for sprouting Instructions)

2 Roma tomatoes

1 Tbsp. chili powder

1 tsp. sea salt

For the topping:

¼ cup **Whipped Avocado Spread**

¼ cup shredded green papaya

2 serrano chilies, diced

½ cup **Sweet and Red Onions**

½ cup diced Hass avocado

1 cup chopped Napa cabbage

1 cup chopped spinach

½ cup **Basic Red Spice Sauce**

To prepare the shells, combine all ingredients in a high-powered blender and blend to a rich, thick mixture. Line a dehydrator tray with a silicone sheet, saran wrap, or a Teflex sheet; and create small circles of mixture 3 inches in diameter and ¼-inch thick. Dehydrate at 118° for 12 hours until crunchy. These will last indefinitely stored in an airtight container. (Makes 16 shells.)

To prepare the topping, place all ingredients except Whipped Avocado Spread in a medium-size mixing bowl and lightly toss together so that fruit and vegetables are well coated in the red sauce.

Coat shells with Whipped Avocado Spread and then layer on fresh topping mixture. This recipe will keep up to 3 days in the refrigerator

Makes 8 servings.

BUCKWHEAT

Buckwheat, the fruit seed of a plant originating in Asia, is a naturally gluten-free grain that is high in protein. It can be sprouted and dried to a great crunchy texture.

Raw buckwheat has many medicinal properties because of its unique composition. It contains vitamins B_1, B_2, B_3, B_5, E, and P; essential amino acids; folic acid, important for pregnant women in particular; magnesium; and manganese. It's also an antitumor grain that helps the liver process hormones and glucose, with the ability to prevent breast cancer and other illnesses associated with hormones. Its properties make it a natural metabolism regulator; a high-energy food, based on its B vitamins alone; and a natural blood-pressure reducer, since it relaxes the blood vessels. With its full chain of amino acids, raw buckwheat decreases cholesterol, too, by eliminating fats. This is an especially good ingredient to work with when beginning to transition your diet. Its nutrient density helps fill you up; it is metabolized slowly, leaving you energized all day long; and it provides important vitamins and minerals.

Working with buckwheat is surprisingly easy. I used to think when I started out raw that any recipe with the word *sprout* in it was going to take a lot of time and be complicated. I didn't know how much I didn't know! Take it from me—it really is easy!

To get started, soak raw hulled buckwheat groats overnight in some water (be sure it's enough to cover the top of them). Leave them covered on the countertop; they don't need refrigeration. After 8–12 hours, rinse well. There will be a gelatinous substance that naturally lifts out of the seeds, and you'll see little tails emerging—that's the sprout! Cover and refrigerate, and use within 2 days.

From a culinary perspective, raw buckwheat will achieve a crunchy texture when dehydrated and makes a great component for snacks, such as crackers, chips, and granolas. This grain takes on the flavor of the ingredients it's mixed with, so it works in many dishes. I find it especially nice in Mexican recipes, like the Tostaditos on the previous page.

FAST AND EASY DESSERTS

Desserts are a joy in the living-foods lifestyle and no longer something to fear in terms of calories and fat content. Most raw desserts are heavy on nuts and fruits, so a little goes a long way, and the nutrient density is much higher than the conventional flour-and-sugar counterparts.

I was born with a sweet tooth, I think, but over time my interest even in *raw* desserts began to calm as my body regained proper balance. Now these recipes are a treat, and I often enjoy them for breakfast (especially the guilt-free chocolate!).

RAINBOW SORBET

Raw sorbets are easy to create and can be made using two different techniques. If you have a Green Star or Champion juicer, you can use frozen fruit and the blank blade. If you don't have a juicer, a blender will work as well, with a little added juice. Here are two flavors to try at home.

For blackberry-peach sorbet:

2 frozen bananas

2 frozen peaches

2 cups frozen blackberries

For mango-raspberry sorbet:

2 frozen bananas

1 cup frozen mango

1 cup frozen raspberries

Pass the various fruits through the juicer, alternating between them. The mixture should come out a perfect sorbet consistency. Garnish with fresh nuts, hemp seeds, coconut, or goji berries.

Makes 2 servings.

KIWI-LIME-STRAWBERRY PARFAIT

Parfaits are great for large families and for events, as they're interactive dishes to prepare. Lay out buffet-style so people can have fun layering to their desired tastes.

2 frozen bananas

2 frozen peeled kiwis

Juice of 1 lime

8 frozen strawberries

2 Tbsp. raw agave nectar or honey

1 cup **Berry Puree**

2 fresh strawberries, chopped

½ cup **Apple-Pistachio Granola** (optional)

In a blender, combine bananas, kiwis, lime juice, frozen strawberries, and sweetener. Blend briefly until well mixed and a rich, creamy frozen sorbet is formed. In a parfait glasses, layer the sorbet first, then chopped berries, and then Berry Puree, finishing with Apple-Pistachio Granola if desired.

Makes 2 servings.

BANANA-CRÈME PIE

This is an easy pie to make, and it sets nicely in the freezer without the need for a dehydrator. It can be made in advance and enjoyed all week long as a tasty treat or even for breakfast!

For the crust:

2 cups raw pecan pieces

½ cup raw honey

1 tsp. cinnamon

For the filling:

2 cups banana

½ cup raw almond butter or pecan butter

1 cup almond milk

½ cup raw honey

1 Tbsp. cinnamon

1 dash nutmeg

1 tsp. sea salt

To prepare crust, pulse the pecan pieces down to a nut meal in a food processor with the S blade in place; then add in cinnamon. From the top, slowly add the sweetener while processing until a dough ball forms. Scrape out dough using a spatula, and set in refrigerator until ready for use.

In a blender, combine all filling ingredients, and puree. Press crust into the bottom of a 10-inch pie container. Once well smoothed over*, top with filling. Place entire pie in the freezer for 4–6 hours before serving. Cut into slices and enjoy with desired garnish.

Makes 10 servings.

*To press down crusts, dip your fingers or a utensil into a bowl of lukewarm water to make spreading easier.

Apple Cobbler

This is a best-selling dessert at 118; it's a comfort food, yet it's guilt free. This cobbler can be made in advance and stored for up to 5 days.

For the filling:

4 cups thinly sliced apples

1 cup raw agave nectar or honey

1 Tbsp. cinnamon

1 tsp. nutmeg

1 tsp. sea salt

For the crust:

4 cups raw pecan or walnut pieces

¾ cup raw agave nectar or honey

1 tsp. cinnamon

1 dash sea salt

To prepare the filling, simply toss the apples, spices, and salt together in a large mixing bowl; coat with desired sweetener. Set aside in the refrigerator, or layer on a covered dehydrator tray and dehydrate at 115° for 15–20 minutes while creating crust.

To prepare crust, pulse the pecan or walnut pieces down to a nut meal in a food processor with the S blade in place; then add in cinnamon and salt. From the top, slowly add the sweetener while processing until a dough ball forms. Remove mixture, setting aside ¼ cup for later use. On a covered dehydrator tray, press out crust into a 5" × 5" square (½" thick) by hand or with a spatula, or shape into a round. Create a small lip around the edge, and top with filling mixture.

On a separate covered dehydrator tray, press out remaining crust mixture to use as topping. Place both trays in the dehydrator at 118° for 2–4 hours. Remove, and gently crumble topping over cobbler. Cut into slices and garnish with dessert sauce (see next section). If you don't have a dehydrator, you can layer the crust and topping in a medium-depth glass dish and refrigerate. (Chill 8 hours prior to serving.)

Makes 8 servings.

PUMPKIN GELATO

Gelato is an easy dish, and this seasonal variety makes use of an underutilized ingredient in the living-foods kitchen. Pumpkin is high in potassium and magnesium, and offers a great flavor profile in desserts, especially during the holiday season.

4 cups diced raw pumpkin

½ cup raw coconut butter

1 cup coconut water or purified water

½ cup raw honey or dates

2 Tbsp. pumpkin-pie spice

1 tsp. sea salt

Pecans for garnish

½ cup **Caramel Sauce**

In a high-powered blender, combine the honey or dates, pumpkin, and water. Blend down to a puree; then add in coconut butter, spice, and salt. Blend to a rich and creamy consistency. Place in a silicone mold in the freezer for best results, and leave for 12 hours to create a nice solid gelato. Garnish with pecans, and enjoy with Caramel Sauce drizzled over the top.

Makes 4 cups.

3 SIMPLE DESSERT SAUCES

Dessert sauces are a must in every living-foods kitchen. Make these in advance and store them in your refrigerator to enjoy throughout the coming weeks—even on plain fruit! When customers are trying to transition to less sugar in their diets, I've seen great results if they have these sauces on hand to satisfy any sweet-tooth cravings that come up.

RICH AND CREAMY CHOCOLATE SAUCE

1½ cups raw cacao powder

1 tsp. cinnamon

1 tsp. vanilla extract or 5 vanilla beans

1 cup raw agave nectar

¼ cup coconut oil or raw coconut butter

1 tsp. Himalayan salt

In a high-powered blender, blend all ingredients until smooth. Add 1 cup nut milk to create a creamy texture and taste that is closer to milk chocolate, if you prefer. This sauce keeps indefinitely and doesn't need refrigeration.

Makes 2 cups.

Caramel Sauce

2 cups raw agave nectar

1 Tbsp. lucuma-root powder

1 Tbsp. mesquite-pod powder

1 Tbsp. maca-root powder

2 tsp. cinnamon

1 tsp. nutmeg

1 tsp. ginger

1 tsp. cloves

1 dash sea salt

Blend all ingredients well or whisk together until rich and creamy. (You can use 2 Tbsp. pumpkin-pie-spice blend as a substitute for the other spices.) This sauce keeps indefinitely and doesn't need refrigeration.

Makes 2 cups.

BERRY PUREE

2 cups fresh strawberries, raspberries, or blackberries

½ cup raw agave nectar or honey

1 tsp. sea salt

¼ cup coconut oil or raw coconut butter (optional)

In a high-powered blender, blend all ingredients until smooth. This sauce keeps for up to 5 days in the refrigerator. Include a mixture of berries to create different flavor profiles. This is a great use for berries that are nearing the end of their freshness date.

Makes 2 cups.

"Children are the world's most valuable resource and its best hope for the future."

— JOHN FITZGERALD KENNEDY

ℱEEDING YOUR FAMILY WELL

Ever since I earned the title "Mom," I've been so concerned about feeding my family well. Many people inquire, "What does your baby eat?" and "What about your husband—is he all raw?" and they're curious what *I* eat at home every day. After living raw for ten-plus years, choosing this option has become easy for me—a necessity, really. I don't feel good otherwise, and health and vitality matter to me.

Naturally, when I found out I was pregnant, I wanted to start learning more about the best choices for my now-growing family. Throughout my pregnancy, I stayed on a raw, vegan diet. We were blessed nine months later with a happy, healthy baby weighing in at eight pounds, two ounces. During my pregnancy, I gained only 20 pounds, and my energy was fantastic. I actually worked right up until the day my son, Dylan, was born; and I never suffered from the complaints I hear of some pregnant women experiencing (constipation, irritability, and so on).

Every pregnancy is different, and it's important to choose what is right for you and your body, but I've learned in my research and through experience that a plant-based, living-foods pregnancy is not only possible, but yields great results if kept in balance. Pregnant and nursing women require a substantial increase in calories, and those calories, chosen correctly, can help create a beautiful life.

Since Dylan arrived, we've stayed raw and primarily vegan, and he is such a balanced baby boy. He's not irritable or fussy in any way; and at two, he has grown into a very healthy, diverse eater. No matter the age of your children, it's possible to encourage them early on to recognize whole, raw foods as being a preferable choice. Weekly, we go as a family to the farmers' market so we can sample the freshest new harvests. Sometimes we head straight to a farm stand and pick juicy fruits and vegetables.

Dylan snacks on buckwheat crisps, drinks green juice and hemp milk, and loves kale salad with dulse! Fruits and vegetables are really the only food groups he knows of, and he seems to be thriving on them.

Feeding a family raw isn't without its challenges, as many of the items you need to stock your pantry with must be made at home by you and your family, requiring some additional time and effort. However, we've found great success by picking a day and making some of our dehydrated items such as granola and crackers for the week and then keeping fresh food always on hand. Kids in particular (adults, too!) will eat whatever is around, so it's important to fill the space with the good stuff. I always keep apples out on the counter within easy reach, as well as other fresh, seasonal fruit. We're even working on growing lettuce in a planter box out back.

This chapter includes a collection of quick recipes my family and I enjoy at home. A little advance planning will help make the transition an easy one in your own kitchen.

If your family has food allergies, there are a couple of suggested substitutions included here. When Dylan was born, he was allergic to many nuts and seeds. I kind of panicked for a moment, being a raw-food chef and aficionado of these ingredients. He was breast-feeding, too, which meant that I would have to forgo these foods as well, in honor of his body's process. But this experience helped me delve deeper into other sources of nutrition within raw foods so I wouldn't have to compromise my family's health in any way.

Hopefully by passing on what I learned for my family, I'll allow *you* to be able to help your loved ones enjoy many raw-food options that will keep them healthy and strong.

SUNSHINE SMOOTHIE

For extra afternoon energy—or some pizzazz in the morning—this treat will get you and your family headed in the right direction. The greens in this drink slow down the metabolism of the fruit sugars and provide sustained energy. Plus, it makes a delicious dessert smoothie!

1 cup raw apple juice or ½ cup fresh berries

1 Tbsp. flaxseed oil

2 Tbsp. supergreens powder

1 leaf of kale or ½ cup spinach

1 banana

1 Tbsp. almond butter or raw coconut butter

1 cup almond milk or **Hemp Milk**

Raw honey or 1 date to sweeten (optional)

Combine allingredients in a basic blender and process on high for 30 seconds until everything, including greens, is well blended. Be sure that the mixture is rich and frothy. If you prefer a cold smoothie, freeze the banana prior to blending or add ½ cup ice.

Makes 16 oz.

WATERMELON ICE

For a treat that's fun to make and even more fun to eat, try this recipe. In the summertime this is a great substitute for the standard Popsicle.

6 cups watermelon, seeds removed

1 Tbsp. raw honey

Combine ingredients in a basic blender and process on high for 30 seconds until all are well blended, forming a thick puree. Set out 2 ice-cube trays and pour in mixture. Freeze 4–6 hours. Before freezing, you may elect to drop some fresh berries into the cubes for added texture.

Makes about 24 ice cubes.

STRAWBERRY CHARD SALAD

Strawberries are a sweet treat providing powerful antioxidants, and taste terrific paired with the natural flavor of chard. Red chard is preferred in this recipe; however, any farm-fresh greens that are soft and supple will work.

For the salad:

2 cups fresh strawberries

8 cups chopped red chard or
    baby greens

1 Reed or Hass avocado, diced

¼ cup sprouted quinoa*

For the dressing:

1 cup extra-virgin olive oil

¼ cup balsamic vinegar

1 clove garlic

1 tsp. sea salt

2 Tbsp. Italian seasoning

2 Tbsp. raw honey

To prepare the dressing, puree all ingredients on high in a high-powered blender until well combined. This dressing will last for up to 14 days in the refrigerator and is delicious with fresh berries. (Makes 1½ cups.)

To finish the salad, toss all remaining ingredients in a large mixing bowl with 1 cup dressing. Split into bowls for serving, and top with additional berries and dressing for garnish.

Makes 4 entrée-size salads.

*To sprout the quinoa seeds, soak in water for 6–8 hours. Rinse well and drain off extra moisture before using. Store excess soaked quinoa in the refrigerator for up to 3 days.

"Fried"-Avocado Mini-Tostadas

We serve this dish at 118, and it's a customer favorite. One day my son, Dylan, came with me to work, and as we walked by the dehydrator, he stopped me and demanded one of the delicious "fried" avocados that top this dish. This is a fun recipe to enjoy with family and friends, and also provides a nutritional boost any time of the day, since it contains several of the powerhouse ingredients that make living foods such a high-energy style of eating: buckwheat, flax, spinach, and avocado.

For the "fried" avocados:

2 large Hass avocados

1 cup extra-virgin olive oil

1 Tbsp. tahini

1 Tbsp. lemon juice

2 cups ground golden flaxseed

1½ Tbsp. sea salt

1 dash cayenne pepper (optional)

For the mini-tostadas:

6 **Tostadito Shells**

1½ cups **Pumpkin-Seed Cheese**

1 cup **Cilantro Sauce**

2 cups julienned cucumbers

½ cup corn

4 cups chopped spinach

1 cup dulse* (optional)

Begin by cutting the avocados in half lengthwise and removing the pits. Slice lengthwise into ½-inch-thick strips and spoon flesh carefully out of skin. In a small bowl, whisk the olive oil, tahini, lemon juice, and 1 tsp. sea salt. Coat the avocado in the oil mixture. On a plate, combine the ground golden flaxseed, remaining salt, and a dash of cayenne, if desired. Coat the avocado carefully, like breading, with the flax mixture, and lay on an uncovered dehydrator tray. Dehydrate at 115° for 4 hours. Dehydrating longer will make for drier avocados, versus a creamier texture after less time. This is a matter of personal preference, and the avocados can be enjoyed even without dehydrating.

To prepare the tostadas, begin by combining the cucumber, spinach, corn, and dulse in a medium-size bowl. Coat well with Cilantro Sauce and set aside for immediate use. Line up Tostadito Shells, top each with ¼ cup Pumpkin-Seed Cheese, and spread evenly. Follow with a layer of ½ cup vegetable mixture, and top with 2–3 "fried" avocado slices each.

Makes 6 mini-tostadas.

*Dulse is a naturally salty treat, and I find that kids actually love it!

FLAXSEED

Flaxseed is one of the only plant sources of ALA, an essential fatty acid, similar to the fatty acids found in fish oils. Flax comes in many colors, ranging from light tan to dark red; and can be found refrigerated as a high-grade supplemental oil and in whole-seed, sprouted, and ground forms. It is recommended that you refrigerate this precious source of omega-3 oils to preserve the nutrient density and integrity of the ingredient. It should be consumed as an oil or ground fresh in order to partake of the many nutritional benefits.

Omega-3s are important to bone health, and flaxseed oil has been proven to reduce the risk of heart disease and lower cholesterol. The essential fatty acid in flax is especially good for pediatric wellness and growing healthy brain tissue, playing a vital role in early development.

CHIPOTLE-RANCH WRAPS

The natural smoky flavor of this dish can be enjoyed by the whole family. The Basic Flax Wraps are relatively quick to prepare, taking only 4–6 hours to dry. They work best when made in a batch of 8, half of which are used in this recipe. The rest can be stored indefinitely in the refrigerator.

For the Basic Flax Wraps:

2 carrots

2 cups ground golden flaxseed

2 cups water

1 Tbsp. sweet chili powder (optional)

1 tsp. sea salt

For the filling:

6 Tbsp. **Smoky Ranchero Sauce**

¼ cup diced mango

1 avocado, diced

2 cups chopped spinach

2 cups diced mushrooms

1 cup corn

¼ cup green onions

To prepare the Basic Flax Wraps, combine the carrots, water, and seasonings in a high powered blender. Blend well until a thick puree forms. Add in the flax and blend until a thick dough mixture forms. Spread over 4 covered dehydrator trays. Make 2 large circles or ovals per tray, spreading to ¼-inch thickness. Dehydrate at 118° for 4–6 hours. To minimize drying time, you may flip the wraps at 3 hours, but be sure to watch closely during the last hours to ensure that the corners don't curl up. (Makes 8 wraps.)

Toss all filling ingredients in a medium-size mixing bowl. Line up 4 wraps on a cutting board; roll tightly around filling and top with additional sauce of choice.

Makes 4 servings.

Rainy-Day Trail Mix

Trail mix is an easy snack to take with you or enjoy while watching your favorite movie on a rainy day! This blend can be made in large batches and saved for that special moment.

For the mixture:

4 cups almonds
  (soaked at least 4 hours)

4 cups **Tostadito Shells**
  (use crumbs and broken pieces)

1 cup dried mission figs
  (soaked to rehydrate)

1 cup buckwheat groats
  (soaked 12 hours)

For the marinade:

¼ cup extra-virgin olive oil

¼ cup raw honey

¼ cup coconut aminos

¼ cup nutritional yeast

1 Tbsp. dried Italian herbs
  or rosemary

1 dash sea salt

1 dash cayenne pepper (optional)

In a medium-size mixing bowl, combine all ingredients and toss well. Layer on a covered dehydrator tray and dehydrate at 118° for 15 hours until mixture is crunchy but figs are still somewhat moist. Store in an airtight container in the pantry indefinitely.

Makes 10 cups.

BASIC PASTAS

Raw pastas are fun and flavorful treats for families to enjoy. Many kids love to eat them according to shape and texture, and squash varieties make a great alternative to standard pasta, especially for gluten-free diets. They may even be served warm straight out of the dehydrator to get a more authentic feel.

Harder gourdlike squashes aren't ideal for pastas, but their softer cousins make a nice pliable noodle. You may combine Italian squash (zucchini), goldbar or crookneck yellow squash, chayote, and others for a lot of color in these dishes. Pastas can be created using a mandoline or Saladacco (garnishing machine). I favor the mandoline—it's easy to use, and the julienne setting gives the noodle a nice weight that is easy to manipulate and won't fall apart.

LEMON-PESTO PASTA

Pesto pasta is nice with a spritz of lemon, served chilled on a summer day; or gently warmed with marinara in the dehydrator as a winter treat.

For the Pesto Sauce:

2 cups fresh basil

1 cup extra-virgin olive oil

1 cup soaked pistachios, walnuts, or pine nuts

6 cloves garlic

1 tsp. sea salt

For the pasta:

4 medium zucchini, julienned

1 lemon

For garnish:

1 cup **Roma-Tomato Marinara** (optional)

Begin by preparing the Pesto Sauce in a high-powered blender. First combine the basil, olive oil, garlic, and salt. Blend on high until a green basil emulsion forms. Add in nuts and continue blending on high until well combined. Pesto will keep for up to 14 days in the refrigerator. (Makes 2 cups.)

In a medium-size bowl, vigorously toss zucchini with 1 cup Pesto Sauce until well coated. Cut the lemon in half and squeeze out juice, toss with pasta, and taste, adding more juice as desired. For a warm treat, top with Roma-Tomato Marinara and place in dehydrator for ½ hour on high before serving.

Makes 4 entrée portions.

SEA VEGETABLES

Dulse, nori, kelp, brown algae, spirulina, and wakame are among a long list of sea vegetables that confer lasting health benefits. These ingredients have a full chain of amino acids; vitamin B_{12}; and trace minerals rarely found in today's food sources, such as zinc, selenium, and chromium. One teaspoon of dried sea vegetables contains 35 milligrams of iron, more than a recommended daily dose, and a high level of vitamin C, which increases the bioavailability of the iron. As a result, sea vegetables naturally regulate blood sugar and heighten immune-system function. Increased energy, improved focus and mental clarity, and healthy blood flow are all by-products of the unique vitamins found in sea vegetables—definitely a great part of a diet composed of living, vital foods.

Sea vegetables can be enjoyed in soups, salads, and sandwiches. Dulse can be munched on alone as a moderately salty snack, and kelp is always a wonderful smoothie ingredient to create a more health-giving tonic.

RASTA PASTA

Kids of all ages love noodles, and this dish is fast and easy to prepare. The toppings are optional, so you can customize this pasta for your own family. We line our toppings up buffet-style on our table so that everyone can pick their favorites!

4 zucchini

1 cup **Pesto Sauce**
  (see previous recipe)

1 cup **Basic Red Spice Sauce**

Juice of 1 lemon

1 tsp. sea salt

Suggested toppings:

Sun-dried tomatoes

Olives

Chopped basil

Avocado

Shredded carrots

Prepare the zucchini by cutting off and discarding the roots and stems. Slice over a mandoline set on the julienne blade to form noodles. In a large bowl, toss with red sauce, pesto, lemon juice, and salt to create the base pasta. Lay out a buffet of toppings, and have fun making a memorable combination each time!

Makes 4 entrée portions.

PASTA ALFREDO

Alfredo is great with a thicker squash noodle or can be enjoyed with kelp noodles—or both in combination.

For the sauce:

2 cups macadamia nuts

I cup coconut water

2 Tbsp. garlic

I tsp. sea salt

2 Tbsp. raw agave nectar or honey

¼ cup extra-virgin olive oil

For the pasta:

8 cups yellow squash or kelp noodles*

I cup diced mushrooms

2 cups spinach

½ cup diced grape tomatoes

½ cup fresh basil

Begin by preparing the sauce in a high-powered blender. Combine all ingredients by loading the blender with liquids first, followed by nuts and spices. Blend on high until a rich, thick dressing forms. The sauce will keep for 4 days in the refrigerator. (Makes 2 cups.)

To finish the dish, toss the noodles with I cup sauce and mushrooms until well combined. Place in dehydrator for ½ hour prior to serving for an even more savory dish. Serve over fresh spinach, which will naturally wilt, softening the greens; and top with grape tomatoes and fresh basil.

Makes 4 entrée portions.

*Kelp noodles are available packaged. To create yellow squash noodles, remove the ends of the squash and julienne using a mandoline.

PLANTING YOUR OWN GARDEN

Planting your own garden is an easy option for growing fresh herbs, lettuce, squash, kale, and tomatoes. You don't need very much space, and you can be harvesting vegetables in as little as two weeks. During our "Farm to Table Culinary Adventures" children's education programs (ages 5–15), facilitated at various school campuses, we grow all of our own produce during the 12-week season as part of the learning process. It's incredible how much we can harvest out of a row of basic planter boxes. We go back and harvest weekly, allowing the plants to regrow in between. The yield from the basic methods of planting can be enough greens and other vegetables for a family of four, no problem. Here are three easy options for planting your own garden:

1. **Plant inside of a planter box or old barrel (about 8–12 inches deep).** To create a simple garden, first line the box or barrel with plastic to insulate the soil. Add in an organic soil compound, filling it to 2 inches from the top. Plant seeds a few inches down into soil, at least 4 inches from one another. Cover with topsoil, and water as needed until seeds begin to grow. One shortcut is to buy a seedling that has already sprouted and cultivate it to a mature plant. Your portable garden can come with you wherever you move, and a smaller version for your kitchen works especially well with basil, rosemary, and mint.

2. **Plant directly into your yard.** To use this technique, prepare the area by tilling the soil and separating it from other encroaching landscape with a plastic or wood barrier to naturally ward off pests and weeds. Till in some fresh organic soil and plant your seedlings or sprouts at least 4 inches deep. Try to line them up 4 inches apart from one another, in overall rows that are at least 8 inches apart. Lettuce, herbs, squash, and root vegetables all grow nicely as row crops. Water as needed, bearing in mind that when plants are producing, they'll need significantly more water to stay well hydrated. Each season, just till the remaining plant back into the earth. Allow one week to season, and replant using the same technique.

3. **Plant in raised planter boxes that have an irrigation system.** These planting systems come complete with irrigation drainage, making monitoring the watering process a little bit easier. These are especially nice in urban areas and can be found at your local hardware store and sometimes through a service that will help with maintenance. These systems will need to be rotated every season. Plant seeds in the same way as in the basic planter boxes, making sure to give the roots time to grow in before harvesting from the plant.

SUNSHINE PASTA

The bright color of this pasta attracts kids without fail. It's a fun combination that delivers 4–5 of the recommended daily servings of vegetables all in one dish.

For the sauce:

4 Roma tomatoes, diced

1 red bell pepper, chopped

1 tsp. raw honey

¼ cup extra-virgin olive oil

1 tsp. sea salt

For the pasta:

8 cups combined zucchini and yellow squash, julienned

1 cup corn

1 cup shredded carrots

1 cup diced tomatoes

Begin by preparing the sauce. Combine vegetables, honey, and salt in a basic blender and puree down to a smooth mixture. (You may have to add up to 2 Tbsp. water to get the blades turning, depending on your blender.) Turn blender on high and slowly add olive oil while blending to emulsify the mixture. (Makes 2 cups.)

To finish, toss together all pasta ingredients with 1 cup sauce until well coated. Garnish with **Raw Parmesan Cheese** and additional fresh vegetables and sauce for more flavor and texture. This dish is best served at room temperature.

Makes 4 entrée portions.

FAMILY-FRIENDLY DESSERTS

Every kid, big or small, loves a treat; and although these sweets still contain natural sugars, they also represent several important food groups, including protein, fruits, and vegetables. Living-foods desserts are fun to prepare as a family and really show kids from an early age that healthy eating can be an enjoyable experience.

ICE-CREAM SLICES

Raw ice cream can actually be considered a meal—high in protein, minerals, and essential vitamins—as well as a decadent treat anytime. Our family keeps a batch on hand, along with fresh fruit; and slicing the ice cream instead of scooping it has proved to be a fun presentation technique that keeps us wanting more! Kids love the triangle shapes, and they can even eat them with their fingers.

2 cups macadamia nuts

¼ cup raw coconut butter

1 cup raw honey or agave nectar

1 tsp. sea salt

2 cups coconut water

1 cup raspberries

Blend all ingredients in a high-powered blender. Pour into a flat glass pie container (8–10 inches round) and place in the freezer for 12 hours. Enjoy a slice with fresh fruit of choice, or top with a dessert sauce from the last chapter. The ice cream keeps indefinitely in the freezer. Makes 8–10 slices.

CACAO-AVOCADO PUDDING

Avocado and chocolate? Yes! This is a nut-free preparation that yields a delicious pudding every time. This recipe is rich and creamy, with a nice soft chocolate flavor, and may be adapted by adding more cacao or nut milk to suit your own needs.

4 Hass avocados

I cup coconut water

½ cup raw honey

I cup raw cacao

I tsp. cinnamon

I tsp. sea salt

Begin by slicing the avocados lengthwise and removing pits. Then scoop out flesh from skins. Combine all ingredients in a blender, loading the liquids first, and blend on high for 30–45 seconds. Scrape out pudding and refrigerate. This recipe keeps for up to 4 days in the refrigerator and is best served chilled.

Makes 3–4 cups, depending on avocado size.

MONKEY BITES

Hands down the best interactive kids' food, this dish is great for parties. The greatest part is, it's a guilt-free dessert, with no preservatives or refined sugars. Most children will love the idea of the bananas alone, but when you add the healthy chocolate and nutrient-dense nuts, you almost have a meal!

For the bites:

1 cup **Rich and Creamy Chocolate Sauce**

4 bananas

8 Popsicle sticks

For the topping:

1 cup dried coconut shreds (unsweetened)

1 tsp. raw honey or agave nectar

½ cup raw nuts of choice (optional)

Begin by peeling the bananas, cutting them in half down the very middle, and sticking them onto Popsicle sticks. Lay out on a plate and place in the freezer briefly (approximately 15 minutes). Meanwhile, combine all topping ingredients in a bowl, toss together, and set aside until time for assembly.

On a table (covered for easier clean-up!), place the chocolate sauce in a bowl that is low and flat enough for dipping. Line up the bananas, the sauce, and the topping, followed by an empty plate. Dip each banana in chocolate; then roll in the topping and set on the empty plate. Place in the freezer for 10–15 minutes and enjoy fresh and chilled.

Makes 8 servings.

APPLE SANDWICHES

Leave this delicious snack on the counter as an after-school treat. The rejuvenating apples are a great afternoon pick-me-up, and the almond butter and flaxseed oil in combination function as great brain food.

4 Gala or Fuji apples

½ cup raw nut butter*

2 Tbsp. raw honey

1 Tbsp. flaxseed oil

1 dash sea salt

Begin by combining the nut butter, honey, flaxseed oil, and sea salt in a small bowl and whisk together. Cut apples into ¼-inch-thick slices (remove the cores). Scoop 2 Tbsp. nut-butter mixture on a piece of apple, spread, and top with another piece of apple. Repeat until all apple slices have become sandwiches.

Makes at least 8 small snack-size sandwiches.

*If you have a nut allergy in the family, try substituting coconut butter or sunflower-seed butter in this recipe.

RAW CUPCAKES

Cupcakes . . . yes! These yummy treats are great for birthdays, social gatherings, and at home as a nice snack. Try one—or all three—of these delicious frostings: pumpkin, chocolate, or vanilla.

For the base:

2 cups dried mission figs
  (soaked to rehydrate)

2 cups pecans

1 cup raw agave nectar or honey

¼ cup psyllium husk

2 Tbsp. cinnamon

1 tsp. nutmeg

1 tsp. sea salt

**For the frosting
  (select from the following):**

Pumpkin

2 cups raw pumpkin

¼ cup raw agave nectar or honey

¼ cup raw almond butter

1 Tbsp. pumpkin-pie spice

1 tsp. sea salt

Chocolate

1 cup raw cacao

¼ cup raw coconut butter

¼ cup raw agave nectar or honey

1 tsp. cinnamon

1 tsp. sea salt

Vanilla

1 cup macadamia nuts

¼ cup raw coconut butter

¼ cup raw agave nectar or honey

¼ cup water (or coconut water)

2 Tbsp. vanilla paste

To prepare the cupcake base, combine soaked figs, spices, psyllium husk, and salt in a food processor. Process to a paste; then add the nuts and continue processing to a thick spread. Last, slowly add the sweetener from the top while processing so that a dough ball begins to form. Stop the processor and scrape out the mixture. Place in a medium-size bowl and refrigerate while preparing frosting.

Combine all ingredients for desired frosting in a high-powered blender. Blend to a thick and creamy consistency. All of the frosting flavors will yield rich pastes, so make sure ingredients are well combined. Refrigerate mixture until ready for use.

To complete the cupcakes, begin by scooping 6 Tbsp. base mixture into a cupcake holder and press down into the mold to create the basic shape. For a drier, more cakelike consistency, at this point you can dehydrate the mixture by placing the mold on an uncovered tray in the dehydrator at 110° for 4 hours. Alternatively, you can freeze the cupcakes for 1 hour until they set. After desired method is performed, remove the cupcakes and spread 2 Tbsp. frosting evenly over the surface of each. Sprinkle with fresh cacao, cinnamon, or coconut shreds for garnish and serve.

Makes 8 cupcakes.

"One cannot think
well, love well, sleep
well, if one has not
dined well."

— VIRGINIA WOOLF

ℰLIXIRS, APPETIZERS, AND SALADS FOR SHARING

Once you're enjoying living foods frequently at home, you'll find that your friends and family may be curious about your newfound attractiveness, energy, and zest for life. For me, people quickly began to notice the benefits of this lifestyle by watching the results I was getting. They detected a particular "glow" and enthusiasm that was very engaging.

Sharing is the best way for loved ones to begin feeling the incredible effects of raw foods, too. It's so natural to want to shout from the rooftops how amazing you feel. The following are some fun recipes to feed your friends that are easy and quick.

Preparing food in large quantities for parties and gatherings will require additional planning and stretch your skills, so I've included tips and tricks to keep your kitchen moving. These dishes are universally enjoyed by folks of all backgrounds, and many don't need much explaining; in fact, it may be better if you don't mention their "raw" nature and let your friends explore on their own.

Eating is done with our eyes first, followed by our stomach, so with each of these recipes, I've included some serving suggestions and fun plating techniques to really spice up the party!

BLUEBERRY LEMONADE

This is an antioxidant, alkaline-forming beverage that proves to be exceptionally refreshing and fun. The berries naturally float atop the elixir and can be served in fluted glasses to toast any special occasion.

½ cup fresh blueberries

2 cups lemon juice

¼ cup raw honey

2 cups coconut water

In a blender, combine the lemon juice, honey, and coconut water. Blend to a frothy elixir. Prepare serving glasses by placing 1 Tbsp. blueberries in each. Pour in liquid, leaving ½ inch of room at the top of each glass. Toss in additional blueberries before serving and toast to your health!

Makes six 6 oz. servings.

LEMON-MINT ICE CUBES

A refreshing addition to any elixir, these flavored ice cubes will catapult your drink presentation to the extraordinary during your next dinner party. Serve these delights in fresh-juice concoctions, or as a garnish to a chilled soup.

4 cups fresh coconut water

¼ cup lemon juice

2 Tbsp. finely chopped fresh mint

2 Tbsp. raw honey (optional)

In a mixing bowl, whisk together all ingredients until a froth begins to form; or place coconut water, lemon juice, and honey in a blender and pulse, whisking in mint afterward. Pour mixture into 3 standard ice-cube trays and freeze.

Makes roughly 36 ice cubes.

GAZPACHO SHOTS

A nice chilled soup, this recipe is perfect for a summer party. Gazpacho shots are a great first-course selection or can be served as a tray-passed appetizer.

2 cucumbers

3 Roma tomatoes

1 red bell pepper

¼ cup basil

1 tsp. sea salt

2 cloves garlic

¼ cup extra-virgin olive oil

Combine all ingredients except olive oil in a blender. Blend on high for 30–45 seconds until vegetable puree is formed. Turn blender on for 15 more seconds and slowly add the oil while blending to emulsify, creating a nice rich soup. Chill for 1 hour before serving. Pour into shot glasses and garnish with some additional basil, shredded carrots, or a slice of red bell pepper for a burst of color.

Makes twelve 2 oz. shots or six 4 oz. appetizer servings.

Mint Juleps

The flavors of the bayou naturally lend themselves to a party, and this beverage is a surprising treat. The coconut oil adds another dimension to aid the digestion of an upcoming meal and slows the metabolism of the fruit sugars.

¼ cup fresh mint

1 honeydew melon

1 Tbsp. coconut oil

2 Tbsp. raw honey or agave nectar

¼ cup raspberries

You can use a blender or juicer to prepare this recipe. If you have a juicer, you'll enjoy a nice rich juice; or in the blender, a thicker, heartier drink emerges. Begin by juicing or blending the honeydew and raspberries. Add the mint, coconut oil, and sweetener to the juicer or blender. If using a blender, blend until well combined; if using a juicer, whisk together after ingredients have all passed through. Pour juice into short glasses, and garnish with additional raspberries on a skewer or mint on the rim. Sit back, relax, and refresh!

Makes 4–6 servings.

MEXI-CALI CHOPPED SALAD

This vegetable chopped salad can be served up fresh alongside any meal and pairs with Latin appetizers like gazpacho and ceviche for a great spread. It's a very basic recipe that highlights the natural flavors of all the ingredients.

2 cups corn

¼ cup stemmed cilantro

2 cups diced cucumber

1 cup diced red onion

¾ cup diced mango

1 cup diced avocado

2 cups diced tomatillos

½ cup **Spicy Pepitas**

Juice of 2 limes

1 cup **Cilantro Sauce**

1 tsp. sea salt

1 dash cayenne pepper

In a large mixing bowl, combine all herbs, vegetables, and fruit (except avocado). Toss with lime juice, Spicy Pepitas, and Cilantro Sauce. Add in sea salt and cayenne, tossing lightly, and then avocado; simply shake the bowl to combine in order to preserve the integrity of the avocado. Using tongs, place salad on chilled small tapas plates or in large coffee mugs for a fun presentation!

Makes 4 servings.

SOBECA SLIDERS

The area where the 118 restaurant is located in Orange County, California, is referred to as the "**S**outh **o**n **B**ristol **E**ntertainment/**C**reative **A**rt" district—Sobeca. This inventive spirit fits well with our food offerings . . . and so these sliders were named. A catering favorite, this basic recipe is easy to re-create at home, and I've enjoyed sharing this fun dish at many special events. These bite-size sandwiches are a delicious combination of olive tapenade, mushrooms, fresh tomatoes, and greens.

For the Buckwheat Buns:

2 cups sprouted buckwheat (for sprouting instructions, see sidebar in Chapter 7)

2 Tbsp. ground golden flaxseed

1 Roma tomato

2 Tbsp. chili powder

1 tsp. sea salt

1¼ cups water

For the filling:

2 large portobello mushrooms

¼ cup balsamic vinegar

2 Roma tomatoes, thinly sliced

2 cups mixed baby greens

1 cup **Sweet and Red Onions**

2 cups **Red Bell Pepper and Olive Tapenade**

To prepare the Buckwheat Buns, begin by blending the tomato, water, chili powder, and sea salt well in a high-powered blender. Add the buckwheat and continue blending until well combined. Add the golden flaxseed and blend on high for 30 seconds. Scrape dough into a bowl. On a covered dehydrator sheet, scoop out 2 Tbsp. mixture at a time, starting in the corner, and continue until you have 4 rows of 4 rounds each. Make sure rounds are about ¼ inch in thickness, and use a spatula to even out. Dehydrate at 118° for 4 hours. Flip buns over and continue dehydrating for 2 more hours until dry to the touch but not crispy.

To prepare the filling, slice the portobello mushrooms lengthwise and toss in a medium-size bowl with the balsamic vinegar until it is absorbed (be careful not to break the mushrooms). Then on a cutting board, lay out Buckwheat Buns and spread a thin layer of tapenade over each one. Layer half of the buns with mixed greens, tomatoes, mushrooms, and onions to create a sandwich-like stack of vegetables. Top each stack with another bun to finish. Serve 2 sliders per plate as an entrée, or arrange on a serving tray to enjoy at a buffet.

Makes 8 sliders.

FOCACCIA 3 WAYS

Focaccia is a fun and easy dish to make. It keeps well and is especially nice warm from the dehydrator. Enjoy the three variations of this recipe with family and friends. Focaccia can even be used as a base for pizzas and pastas.

For the bread:

4 cups sprouted Kamut or rye

¼ cup extra-virgin olive oil

1 tsp. sea salt

1 clove garlic

For the focaccia flavor (select from the following):

Sweet-Onion Focaccia

2 cups **Sweet and Red Onions**

2 cups thinly sliced Roma tomatoes

1 tsp. sea salt

1 Tbsp. dried Italian seasoning

Olive and Garlic Focaccia

2 cups diced, pitted kalamata olives

¼ cup minced garlic

3 Tbsp. **Red Bell Pepper and Olive Tapenade**

Basil and Red Bell Pepper Focaccia

4 cups thinly sliced red bell peppers

¼ cup dried basil

¼ cup extra-virgin olive oil

1 tsp. sea salt

To prepare the bread, process the sprouted grain down to a paste in a food processor with the S-blade attachment. Add the olive oil, garlic, and salt while processing until a dough ball forms. Gently lay out on a covered dehydrator tray. Spread to ⅓-inch thickness using warm water on a spatula, if necessary, to get an even, flat surface. Dehydrate at 118° for 2 hours. Flip bread over; the newly exposed side will still be damp. Set aside to cool.

In a medium-size mixing bowl, combine all ingredients for desired focaccia flavor. Spread the mixture over the soft top of bread and press down so that it becomes part of the dough. Dehydrate for 2–4 more hours, until desired softness is achieved. Refrigerate for up to 5 days. For quick and easy appetizers, cut bread into quarters, and further divide each quarter into 4 triangle shapes.

Makes 1 full tray.

COCONUT-MANGO CEVICHE

Marinated ceviches like this one can be made in advance and stored for up to a week before sharing with family and friends. The flavor actually becomes stronger the longer the mixture is allowed to marinate. Serve this as an appetizer or a meal alongside guacamole and chips.

4 Roma tomatoes, diced

2 cups coconut flesh

1 mango, diced

½ cup lemon juice

¼ cup cilantro

¼ cup green onions

1 tsp. sea salt

2 Tbsp. chili powder

In a large mixing bowl, toss tomatoes with the mango, lemon juice, chili powder, and salt. Chop herbs down to small-to-midsize pieces and toss into bowl. Prepare the coconut flesh by rinsing in lukewarm water to ensure all husk residue has been removed. Layer the flat pieces on a cutting board and slice lengthwise in strips that are ¼–½ inch in thickness. Add to bowl. Toss mixture well until all pieces are evenly coated in spices and liquid; then refrigerate for at least 1 hour prior to serving (keeps refrigerated for up to 7 days). For a fun presentation, serve in martini glasses lined with **Tostadito Shells,** with avocado for garnishing.

Makes 4 cups.

COCONUT-CURRY ROLLS

These rolls make a colorful display and are a delicious treat for any event. They can be cut down to appetizer portions or left whole to be served as an entrée. Plated with your choice of dipping sauce, this dish can easily be adjusted to accompany many styles of meals.

For the wraps:

2 cups coconut flesh

½ cup ground golden flaxseed

¼ cup curry powder

I tsp sea salt

I cup coconut water

For the filling:

I cup chopped red chard

2 cups diced seasonal vegetables of choice (red bell peppers, carrots, green onions, and green papaya)

I cup shredded carrots

2 cups diced avocado (bathed in a small amount of lemon juice to preserve color)

Plan to prepare the wraps in advance. To begin, combine all ingredients except ground flaxseed in a high-powered blender and blend to a thick puree (make sure coconut flesh is cleaned very well beforehand). Add flax and blend another 25–30 seconds. Spread mixture over covered dehydrator tray at ¼-inch thickness; then dehydrate at 115° for 6 hours. When ready to be removed, the wraps will be pliable and not crispy. Be sure to watch the mixture the last hour to ensure that it doesn't become overly dry. Remove from tray and cut down into 8 pieces that can be easily rolled.

Right before serving the rolls, prepare filling. Line a cutting board with dried wraps; then fill each center with 2 Tbsp. chopped red chard to start. Top with ¼ cup seasonal vegetable mixture in a straight line over chard, then 2 Tbsp. shredded carrots over vegetables, and finally ¼ cup diced avocado. Roll wrap tightly around mixture and secure with sandwich pick. Serve each roll with dipping sauce of choice (the **Coconut-Curry Sauce, Cilantro Sauce,** and **Basic Red Spice Sauce** are all great dips).

These rolls can be made in advance. Be aware, though, that the red chard layer serves to keep the wrap from absorbing moisture from the vegetables inside. Prior to rolling, it's very important that there isn't any moisture runoff, to maintain the integrity of the wraps as they sit.

Makes 8 rolls.

SQUASH RAVIOLI

Squash ravioli are a great tray-passed appetizer and a surefire party pleaser; plus, they're fun to make with the whole family. I like to have them on hand in my own kitchen as a go-to snack, and they're easy to create in large quantities. These ravioli are deceptively small, yet very filling!

4 cups thinly sliced zucchini
   (⅛- to ¼-inch-thick rounds)

2 cups macadamia nuts

1 cup water

2 Roma tomatoes

2 Tbsp. extra-virgin olive oil

¼ cup lemon juice

2 cloves garlic

1 tsp. sea salt

2 cups fresh chopped spinach

Roma-Tomato Marinara for garnish

To prepare the filling, combine all ingredients except zucchini and spinach in a high-powered blender until rich and creamy. Pour mixture into a medium-size mixing bowl and then fold in spinach.

Set mixture aside and begin to prepare ravioli by laying zucchini rounds on a dehydrator tray. Then scoop 2 Tbsp. filling mixture onto each round. Top with another zucchini round and garnish with a dot of Roma-Tomato Marinara. Dehydrate at 118° for 2 hours. Remove, and let cool briefly; serve warm. If no dehydrator is available, these ravioli may be placed in the oven at a low temperature, allowing the door to stay open.

Makes 2 dozen ravioli.

OLIVE OIL

Mediterranean cultures widely use olive oil as a standard culinary option, as well as an elixir of youth. Raw oils promote healthy hair, skin, and nails from within—especially olive oil, due to its high level of polyphenols and ability to insulate the cell wall, keeping it at an optimal level to absorb nutrients from the bloodstream.

Extra-virgin or cold pressed olive oils have been minimally processed and not heated, which compromises the nutritional benefits of the oil. The FDA recommends 2 tablespoons a day for cardiovascular health. Olive oil lowers the risk of heart disease by reducing the LDL (low-density lipoprotein) cholesterol levels in the blood.

MUSHROOMS WITH WILD ARUGULA ON PORTOBELLO CRISPS

This recipe is rich in flavor, with key ingredients of truffle-infused oil and garlic. Perfect for evening entertaining and dressed-up functions, this small plate can be made in advance the day before and just warmed before serving.

For the marinated mushrooms:

4 cups sliced cremini mushrooms

I cup sliced shiitake mushrooms

2 Tbsp. truffle oil

2 Tbsp. capers

I Tbsp. minced garlic

¼ cup extra-virgin olive oil

I tsp. raw honey

I cup chopped basil

2 cups wild arugula

For the crisps:

I portobello mushroom

2 cups dark ground flaxseed

2 Tbsp. dried Italian seasoning

I cup water

I Roma tomato

Plan to prepare the crisps in advance. First, combine all ingredients except ground flaxseed in a high-powered blender and blend down to a puree. Add flax and continue blending until a thick mixture forms. Spread mixture quickly and evenly (¼-inch thickness) onto a covered dehydrator sheet. Score into desired shapes (triangles, squares, or circles). Dehydrate at 118° for 12 hours or until crispy. (Makes 12–16 crisps.)

To prepare the marinated mushrooms, combine all ingredients except chopped basil, capers, and arugula in a medium-size mixing bowl. Toss until well coated and oil is absorbed into mushrooms. Dehydrate mixture on a lined dehydrator sheet at 118° for 40 minutes. Remove; while still warm, toss with basil, capers, and arugula. Top each crisp with 2 Tbsp. mixture, or place in a bowl with crisps on the side.

Makes at least 8 servings.

STACKED SWEET NOODLES

Sweet noodles can be prepared as an entrée, side dish, or appetizer. You can make a large batch and use a compression mold to create a stacked effect prior to serving. Surprisingly filling, this dish can be enjoyed warm or cold depending on the time of year.

For the noodles:

2 zucchini

2 yellow squash

¼ cup dulse

1 avocado, diced

2 dates, diced

For the sauce:

2 cups macadamia nuts

1 cup coconut water

1 Roma tomato

¼ cup extra-virgin olive oil

2 Tbsp. raw honey or 2 dates

1 tsp. sea salt

¼ cup chopped basil

1 clove garlic

1 portobello mushroom, diced

2 Tbsp. chili powder

First, prepare the noodles by julienning the vegetables on a mandoline and placing noodles in a large mixing bowl. Add in avocado, dulse (pulled apart into bite-size pieces), and dates.

Prepare the sauce in a blender by combining all ingredients except basil and mushrooms. Blend on high for 30 seconds or until a thick puree forms and the mixture is clearly well combined. Pour sauce little by little into bowl with pasta, tossing vigorously at intervals. When well sauced, add the basil and mushrooms. Toss well to finish. Use a compression mold to create delightful height and presentation, and garnish with additional chiffonaded basil.

Makes 4–6 servings.

Enticing Entrées
and Desserts for
Potlucks and
Dinner Parties

Dinner parties and potlucks are my favorite way to share living foods with family and friends. The beauty and flavor of the dishes never fail to amaze guests, as most people think that healthy fare has to be dull and boring. These party-pleasing recipes are great conversation pieces. The best part about sharing this fun food with family and friends is knowing that it's a nourishing offering that will truly do a body good.

LAYERED VEGETABLE DISHES

Layered vegetable dishes are easy to create in large quantities and can be enjoyed immediately or stored until the next day, making advance preparation a possibility when entertaining or taking food to a gathering. These dishes are guaranteed crowd-pleasers and can be served warm or at room temperature. They may be made in full sheets and cut down easily into desired serving sizes, depending on the style of event.

5-VEGETABLE LASAGNA

Layers of fresh seasonal vegetables, delicious macadamia-squash crème filling, and savory spices add up to a tasty dish for any occasion.

For the filling:

2 cups macadamia nuts

1 cup water

1 cup diced butternut squash

2 Tbsp. dried Italian seasoning

2 Roma tomatoes

½ cup lemon juice

2 cloves garlic

1 tsp. sea salt

2 Tbsp. extra-virgin olive oil

For the layers:

4 heirloom tomatoes, cut on a bias

6 zucchini

4 cups chopped chard

6 portobello mushrooms, cut lengthwise

To prepare the filling, blend all ingredients in a high-powered blender to a thick puree, making sure the crème is well combined. A smooth sauce makes a big difference in this dish.

To prepare the lasagna, first cut the zucchini lengthwise into paper-thin strips (⅛-inch thickness) using a mandoline. Layer barely overlapping pieces on a covered dehydrator sheet or a sheet pan (if you don't plan to dehydrate). Fill the tray, or divide in individual portions, depending on final serving needs. Top the zucchini with ½-inch-thick layer of filling mixture. Cover with a layer of heirloom tomatoes and then a well-spaced layer of portobello mushrooms; follow with a layer of chopped chard. Top with another layer of zucchini. Repeat, forming 2 identical sets of layers. Garnish with dried Italian seasoning or **Roma-Tomato Marinara.**

If not using a dehydrator, refrigerate and enjoy as needed. The longer the mixture sits, the more flavorful the dish will become. If using a dehydrator, set at 118° and leave in for 4 hours. Remove when ready, pour off any excess moisture, and serve immediately. The longer the filling stays in the dehydrator, the more "set up" it will be. Refrigerate leftovers for 1 additional day.

Makes 6–8 entrée portions.

EGGPLANT STACKS

Layers of eggplant, tahini paste, and fresh greens give rise to a colorful and rich Mediterranean-inspired combination. Enjoy this dish immediately, or after a short time in the dehydrator for additional flavor.

For the filling:

2 cups tahini paste

1 Tbsp. miso paste

1 cup lemon juice

2 cloves garlic

1 tsp. sea salt

¼ cup parsley

For the layers:

6 cups chopped chard

½ cup chopped parsley

2 large eggplants, thinly sliced into rounds (roughly 4 cups)

½ cup **Sweet Miso Dressing**

To prepare the filling, begin by combining the lemon juice, garlic, parsley, and salt in a food processor with the S-blade attachment. Process ingredients until well combined; then with the processor still running, slowly pour in tahini and miso pastes. Process briefly until combined but not green from herbs, allowing some pieces to remain. Set aside for immediate use.

To prepare the layered stacks, toss the eggplant rounds in a medium-size bowl with the Sweet Miso Dressing until theysoak up the dressing. In a separate bowl, combine the chard, parsley, and 2 cups filling; fold together to create a thick mixture. On a cutting board, lay out ⅓ of the eggplant rounds. Top each with 2 Tbsp. filling, ¼ cup chard mixture, and another layer of eggplant rounds. Repeat, forming 2 identical sets of layers. Enjoy immediately, or dehydrate at 118° for 2 hours and serve warm.

Makes 10–12 servings.

HEIRLOOM-TOMATO TERRINE

A terrine is a special type of layered dish that is achieved by pressing the ingredients together. This recipe can be prepared in advance and placed in the dehydrator the day of an event for great results.

For the savory crust:

1 cup walnuts

1 cup **Basic Vegetable Stock**

1 tsp. sea salt

¼ cup extra-virgin olive oil

For the layers:

6 heirloom tomatoes, cut into ¼-inch-thick round slices

6 yellow crookneck squash, sliced lengthwise into thin strips (⅛-inch thickness)

3 cups **Stuffed Mushrooms**

First prepare the crust. In a food processor with the S-blade attachment, pulse nuts down to a meal; pour in vegetable stock, salt, and oil; and process until a dough ball forms. This crust is great for savory pies and in stuffed and layered vegetable dishes, so if you'll be preparing for large groups often, feel free to make multiple crusts and store in the refrigerator for up to 2 weeks.

To complete the terrine, line a Bundt-pan mold or similar container (cheesecake molds work great, too) with saran wrap or parchment paper. Begin by creating an overlapping layer of yellow squash. Cover the surface of the squash with heirloom tomatoes. Top with 1½ cups Stuffed Mushrooms. Repeat layers. Gently press together, applying moderate pressure. Finish with a layer of savory-crust mixture. Place entire mold in dehydrator and dehydrate at 118° for 4 hours. If not dehydrating, place in the refrigerator and let stand 24 hours. When the recipe is set up, invert the mold onto a cutting board and carefully pull out the saran wrap or parchment paper. Cut terrine into ½- to 1-inch slices and enjoy. Garnish with additional sauces, if desired, or chopped fresh herbs.

Makes 8–10 thin slices.

STUFFED-VEGETABLE DISHES

Stuffed vegetables are especially nice at the height of the season, when tomatoes or peppers are at the peak of flavor. Use as an entrée or side dish when entertaining.

These recipes are easy to prepare in large quantities and keep for up to five days in the refrigerator. Stuffed-vegetable dishes travel well and hold up for a few days at a time, making advance preparation a little bit simpler. These recipes can also be easily adapted to accommodate the change in seasons by shifting the sauce or vegetables inside.

STUFFED MUSHROOMS

This is a nice dish to bring along to potlucks, and depending on the size of the mushrooms you decide to stuff, can make for quick one-bite snacks, perfect for tray passing.

4 cups cremini mushrooms (medium to large stems) or 4 large portobello mushrooms

For the filling:

1 cup basil

1½ cups pistachios or pecans

4 cloves garlic

1 red bell pepper

¼ cup sun-dried tomatoes

¾ cup extra-virgin olive oil

1 tsp. sea salt

Begin by preparing the filling. Blend the olive oil, basil, garlic, and sea salt well in a basic blender. After a rich emulsion forms, add in the nuts of choice and blend well until a thick paste forms. Chop the sun-dried tomatoes evenly and fold into mixture. Slice the red bell pepper lengthwise and remove stem and seeds. Dice down to ⅛-inch pieces and add to filling mixture.

In a medium-size mixing bowl, toss the mushrooms (after de-stemming and wiping clean with a damp cloth) with a little olive oil until lightly coated. Then on a covered dehydrator tray, arrange mushrooms concave side up so that they are barely touching one another. Fill mushroom caps evenly with filling. Dehydrate at 118° for 4 hours. Enjoy topped with additional nuts, marinara, or dried herbs.

Makes 16 small to midsize, or 4 entrée-size, mushrooms.

STUFFED HEIRLOOM TOMATOES

To preserve as much decadent flavor as possible, this recipe uses the entire to-mato in one way or another—nothing goes to waste. While heirloom varieties are only available for a short time twice yearly, Roma tomatoes are more readily obtain-able throughout the year and make a good substitution in this recipe.

6 heirloom tomatoes

For the filling:

Heirloom-tomato hearts (removed during tomato preparation)

2 cups diced mushrooms

½ cup chopped basil

2 cups chopped spinach

2 cups walnut meal*

2 cups **Pesto Aioli**

To prepare the tomatoes for stuffing, remove tops by carefully slicing ¼ inch down from stem and across. Using a cor-ing device or ice-cream scoop, remove the tomato hearts and place to the side for use in filling.

To prepare the filling, pulse together the mushrooms, tomato hearts, and basil in a food processor with the S-blade at-tachment. After these ingredients are well combined, add in walnut meal and briefly pulse again. Remove mixture from the food processor and set aside. Then in a medium-size mixing bowl, combine Pesto Aioli and chopped spinach. Toss together well so greens are coated with sauce.

Begin layering the mixtures inside of the tomatoes. Alternate between the two, loading in about 2 Tbsp. of each, until tomato is filled. Replace tops. Place the tomatoes in a casserole dish in the refrigerator and let sit 4 hours prior to serving; or place on a dehydrator sheet and dehydrate on high for 2 hours, lower to 118°, and continue dehyrating for an additional 2 hours. If dehydrating, enjoy right away, garnishing with **Marinated Mushrooms,** if desired. Allow leftovers to cool, and refrigerate to enjoy the fol-lowing day.

Makes 6 tomatoes.

*To prepare walnut meal, gently pulse raw, unsoaked walnuts down to a fine powder in a food processor using the S-blade attachment.

STUFFED RED BELL PEPPERS

This Latin-inspired dish with smoky sauce is a great addition to a meal or can stand alone. Enjoy it the following day for even more flavor. You can also substitute pasilla chilies for the red bell pepper to create spicy poppers.

4 red bell peppers
(or spicy pasilla chilies)

For the filling:
2 cups **Smoky Ranchero Sauce**
2 cups corn
2 cups shredded chayote squash
2 cups diced tomatoes

For garnish:
2 cups **Tomatillo Salsa**
2 cups **Whipped Avocado Spread**

To prepare the peppers (or chilies) for stuffing, cut off the stems ¼ inch from the top, slice lengthwise, and remove and discard all seeds inside. Set aside until filling is ready. If planning to dehydrate, let sit in a little bit of olive oil to soften skins.

In a medium-size mixing bowl, combine filling ingredients and toss well. Lay pepper halves on a cutting board and fill with ½–¾ cup mixture each. Place all filled pepper halves on a covered dehydrator sheet and dehydrate at 118° for 4 hours. Remove, and garnish with 2 Tbsp. Tomatillo Salsa and 2 Tbsp. Whipped Avocado each before serving.

Makes 8 servings.

STUFFED AVOCADOS

This can be a festive dish for holiday parties or a school event. Hass avocados are the preferred choice for stuffing, and can be made sweet or savory depending on the toppings you choose. (Stuffed avocados are best enjoyed fresh.)

4 avocados

**For the filling
(select from the following):**

Sweet

½ cup pomegranate seeds and/or dried cranberries

2 cups diced apples

2 cups **Smoky Ranchero Sauce**

2 cups chopped spinach

Savory

½ cup walnuts

2 cups diced cucumber

2 cups **Whipped Avocado Spread**

2 cups finely chopped kale

To prepare the avocados for stuffing, slice lengthwise and remove pits. Scoop out half of soft flesh using a fruit scoop or a spoon, leaving a small layer still attached inside the skin. Dice the removed avocado flesh and set aside.

In a medium-size mixing bowl, combine all ingredients for chosen filling and toss so the mixture is well combined. Lay out avocados, and top evenly with mixture. Finish by garnishing with the fresh diced avocado. If you're making this dish in advance, spritz a little lemon or lime juice over the garnish to keep it looking bright green. Sprinkle with a gourmet salt right before serving to enhance flavor and add color.

Makes 8 servings.

Desserts are an easy way to introduce friends and family to living foods, as most people have a bit of a sweet tooth. These recipes are perfect for group celebrations and holiday potlucks. Raw desserts have several functional-food properties, while still being a tasty treat, and are fun to present in a combination platter during an event.

CHOCOLATE-BERRY TACOS

This is a delectable dish that is so fun to look at, you almost don't want to eat it! Fresh berries are wrapped in a chocolate taco shell, coated with delicious frosting . . . yum!

For the taco shells:

1 cup sprouted buckwheat (for sprouting instructions, see sidebar in Chapter 7)

¼ cup dark flaxseed

½ cup cacao

¼ cup raw agave nectar

1 Tbsp. cinnamon

1 tsp. sea salt

1 tsp. vanilla

For the filling and topping:

1½ cups **Vanilla Frosting**

1½ cups **Chocolate Frosting**

3 cups fresh mixed berries

To prepare taco shells, begin by blending all ingredients well in a high-powered blender. When a nice thick puree is formed, transfer batter to a container that is easy to pour from. Line a dehydrator sheet with Teflex, parchment, or silicone. Pour out ¼ cup mixture per serving, and press into circular shape 4 inches in diameter and ¼-inch thick; repeat until tray is full, making sure the edges barely touch. Dehydrate at 118° for 6 hours until dry but still flexible. Remove from dehydrator sheet and store in the refrigerator until ready for use. (Makes 12 shells.)

To complete the taco preparation, line up shells flat on a cutting board and spread on 2 Tbsp. Vanilla Frosting each to within ¼ inch of edge. Top with ¼ cup fruit filling each. Roll tightly around mixture or fold in half, and top with 2 Tbsp. Chocolate Frosting per taco. Serve on a platter, with extra berries for garnish.

Makes 12 tacos.

MACADAMIA MACAROONS

A 118 favorite, these treats are great as a breakfast snack or a dessert, taste delicious with smoothies or coffee drinks, and are the hit of every party. Enjoy these scrumptious, simple cookies year-round.

4 cups raw macadamia nuts

1½ cups raw honey or agave nectar

2 Tbsp. maca-root powder

1 tsp. sea salt

1 cup coconut shreds (unsweetened)

Begin by combining the coconut shreds and 2 Tbsp. sweetener in a small bowl. Toss so shreds are well coated but not clumped together. To prepare the basic dough, place the macadamia nuts in a food processor with the S-blade attachment and process down to a meal or flourlike consistency; then add the maca-root powder and sea salt and blend. Finally, slowly add the remaining sweetener while processing until a dough ball forms. Remove from processor and place in a medium-size bowl. Scoop out into 1-inch balls and roll in coconut mixture, pressing shreds into dough until well formed.

Place the macaroons on an uncovered dehydrator sheet and dehydrate at 118° for 6–8 hours, until desired consistency is achieved. If you don't have a dehydrator, these are equally enjoyable without drying, but the result will be more chewy. If a more solid cookie is desired, the mixture may be frozen for an hour prior to serving. Garnish with **Chocolate Frosting** or **Berry Puree.**

Makes 1 dozen cookies.

CHOCOLATE-FUDGE EASY BROWNIES
(NO-BAKE, OF COURSE!)

These treats can be prepared in minutes and enjoyed in no time at all. No-bake brownies are a healthy way to satisfy any sweet tooth. Great for last-minute events, this recipe can be prepared in large batches or cut down to bite-size pieces easily.

2 cups raw dates

1 cup raw cacao

¼ cup raw almond butter

1 tsp. cinnamon

1 dash sea salt

2½ cups **Chocolate Frosting**

Combine all ingredients except frosting in a food processor with the S-blade attachment. Process the dough to a rich, creamy consistency that still has enough body to be shaped. Press mixture into a 5 inch-deep baking dish greased with a little bit of coconut oil. Coat top with an even layer of frosting. Freeze for 10 minutes, or refrigerate for 20 minutes. Cut into desired shapes and enjoy!

Makes an average of twelve 2" × 2" brownies.

BASIC DESSERT BARS

This recipe is easy to create in large batches, perfect for playdates and get-togethers. These bars can be saved for up to 2 weeks and enjoyed any time of the day. Choose between refreshing citrus and strawberry-shortcake toppings.

For the bar base:

4 cups macadamia nuts

2 Tbsp. raw coconut butter

¾ cup raw agave nectar or honey

1 Tbsp. vanilla paste

1 tsp. sea salt

**For the topping
  (select from the following):**

Citrus

4 Meyer lemons, peeled

½ cup raw agave nectar

1 Tbsp. raw coconut butter

1 Tbsp. psyllium husk or Irish moss

1 tsp. sea salt

Strawberry shortcake

4 cups fresh strawberries

½ cup **Berry Puree**

¼ cup raw honey

1 dash sea salt

Begin by preparing the bar base. In a food processor with the S blade in place, process the macadamia nuts down to a meal. Add in all additional ingredients except sweetener and process until well combined. Add in sweetener while processor is running and stop as soon as a dough ball begins to form. Place mixture in a large glass tray and spread out to ½-inch thickness. Freeze while preparing topping.

For citrus topping:

Combine all ingredients in a high-powered blender and blend until a thick paste is formed. Remove from blender and spread over bar base immediately. Freeze for 2 hours prior to serving.

For strawberry-shortcake topping:

Cut strawberries into quarters and place in a bowl; toss with other ingredients. Using a spatula, break down berries until a loose-chop topping forms. Spread mixture over bar base (frozen at least 2 hours) right before serving.

Makes 12 servings.

"As your understanding of life continues to grow, you can walk upon this planet safe and secure, always moving forward toward your greater good."

— LOUISE HAY

TRANSITION FOODS

Changing your diet occurs one day—one bite—at a time. Each moment reflects the transition to a more vibrant lifestyle, and it's important to honor all aspects of this process and how they manifest for you. Maybe you've been successful with raw breakfasts and everyday lunchtime items, and now you're interested in incorporating more living foods into your evening meals. Oftentimes while in transition, people are still looking to eat some cooked foods and are concerned about proper combinations.

Eating whole foods is always the best choice. Here is a simple check-in: Periodically look at what you're consuming and ask, *Is this a whole food?* For example, quinoa is a whole grain, but a store-bought tortilla, in contrast, must be processed first, is usually made from an enriched flour, and contains multiple ingredients. If in the process of transitioning your diet, you're still enjoying some cooked items, be sure to make them *whole* ones.

Cooking preparation makes a big difference, too. Steaming vegetables and grains is the optimal technique for maintaining the ingredients' nutritional value. Sautéing isn't the best choice, as the high heat and oil associated with this cooking method create toxins in the dish. However, it's possible to steam some broccoli, for instance, and then add *raw* oil or sauce to enjoy greater health benefits. Cooked oils are one of the hardest toxins for the body to process, getting stored in vital organs like the gallbladder, and must be "cleansed" out. On the other hand, if you add raw oils to lightly steamed veggies, those oils are still molecularly sound and full of enzymes, and will aid in the digestion of the accompanying food.

Another good alternative is baking instead of frying. It's possible to cook yams in the oven—serving them with fresh, raw vegetables and sauces—and still enjoy many of the essential vitamins and nutrients inherent in the starch.

Taking all of this into account, here are some easy recipes that incorporate many raw components with cooked items, and will help you in the transition to a more vibrant diet and optimal health.

ASPARAGUS AND ONION SPLIT-PEA SOUP

Hearty and satisfying, this soup can be enjoyed as a meal or side dish. The secret to "transitional" soups is adding the raw oil at the end so that you still enjoy all of its health benefits. This is a family recipe that is high in protein, as well as vitamins A and C.

1 large sweet onion
8–10 medium asparagus stalks
2 cups dried split peas
3 cups vegetable stock (oil free)
1 tsp. Himalayan salt
¼ cup extra-virgin olive oil

Slice onion in half lengthwise and then cut down into smaller pieces. Break asparagus in half, and in a medium saucepan, combine with the onion and all other ingredients except olive oil. Place over stove on medium heat and bring to a boil. Turn down to a simmer and cover. Let simmer for 30 minutes. Turn off burner and remove from heat. Using a handheldred blender, carefully blend the soup to a rich, thick, creamy mixture; then add in the oil while blending—this will help to emulsify the soup, making it even creamier.

Makes 4 entrée servings.

BUDDHA'S BOWL

At 118, we serve this dish completely raw, and it has proved to be very popular. It's easy to translate into a transitional dish by adding a steamed grain of choice. This recipe is the perfect balance of greens and other colorful fruits and vegetables, providing sustained energy for a full day.

4 cups chopped red chard

2 cups julienned yellow crookneck or goldbar squash

½ cup red grapes, halved

¼ cup diced red bell peppers

¼ cup sprouted Kamut or spelt, or 1 cup steamed grain of choice

½ cup Coconut-Curry Sauce

In a medium-size bowl, toss red bell peppers, squash, and grain with sauce until all ingredients are well coated. In serving bowls, layer red chard, then grain mixture. Garnish with red grapes on top and additional sauce, if desired.

Makes 2 entrée portions.

CILANTRO-RICE DISH

When my son was a newborn and we were in the process of diagnosing his allergies, rice was an agreed-upon "safe" item for us to eat, as rice allergies run very low. This is also a nice transition food, since it contains no gluten, and if you choose to enjoy dark brown or black varieties, there are many health benefits to be derived from the grain itself. For this dish, I suggest a brown basmati rice, if possible—the grain is longer and steams to a nice and fluffy consistency.

For the Cilantro Sauce:

1 cup extra-virgin olive oil

2 Tbsp. lemon juice

1 clove garlic

¼ cup stemmed cilantro

1 tsp. sea salt

For the dish:

2 cups cooked basmati rice

1 cup shredded carrots

1 cup chopped green onions

1 cup assorted raw vegetables of choice (I recommend julienned squash and cubed avocado)

Combine all sauce ingredients in a basic blender and puree to a dark green color. In a large bowl, toss rice and all vegetables. Add the sauce to the mixture a little at a time until well coated. Let sit a few minutes to cool. The heat from the rice isn't enough to cook the vegetables or the oil-based Cilantro Sauce. As a result, this dish is easy to digest and high in enzymes even though it contains the cooked rice.

Makes 4 servings.

QUINOA BBQ BOWL

Quinoa is an ancient grain that is gluten free and contains 14 grams of protein per ½-cup serving. It can be enjoyed raw or cooked with great results, and is a helpful ingredient when transitioning to a plant-based diet because of its high protein content.

For the BBQ sauce:

4 dates

2 Tbsp. chili powder

2 Tbsp. coconut aminos (optional)

1 tsp. sea salt

2 tomatoes

1 red bell pepper

½ clove garlic

For the bowl:

2 cups cooked quinoa

1 cup raw corn

2 cups lightly steamed cauliflower

1 cup diced portobello mushrooms

½ cup thinly sliced red onions

To prepare the sauce, combine all ingredients in a high-powered blender and blend well until a thick sauce forms. Set aside.

To prepare the bowl itself, begin by tossing the portobello mushrooms and red onions with 2 Tbsp. BBQ sauce until all are well coated. Add in the corn and cauliflower, and toss all ingredients well. In serving bowls, layer steamed quinoa, then vegetable mixture. Drizzle with remaining BBQ sauce and enjoy!

Makes 2 entrée portions.

STUFFED YAMS

Yams are very high in iron and are an excellent source of potassium. Steamed or baked ones make a great base for this dish; sweet potatoes may be used as well. The main goal is to go with whole foods direct from the earth, and this recipe features some delectable root vegetables, known for being very grounding and providing balance.

For the sauce:

1 cup raw tahini

1 clove garlic

1 tsp. sea salt

1 Tbsp. chili powder

1 tsp. dark raw honey

½ tsp. cinnamon

1 cup carrot juice or
 2 Roma tomatoes

For the dish:

2 four- to six-inch yams

1 cup broccoli

1 cup diced green beans

Begin by blending sauce ingredients in a basic blender. Steam or bake yams and steam other vegetables until tender. Slice yams lengthwise, and mash flesh briefly to a coarse texture. Then fill each half with ½ cup vegetables atop the mash. Drizzle with sauce and enjoy.

Makes 2 entrée portions.

VEGETABLE COCONUT-CURRY DISH

Curry is a naturally warming blend of spices, and this recipe is a family favorite during the cold months. The turmeric in the yellow curry helps boost memory and brain function, as well as being good for the heart.

1 cup cauliflower

1 cup broccoli

1 cup snap peas

1 cup diced carrots

1 cup diced asparagus
   (stems discarded)

¼ cup pomegranate seeds (optional)

2 cups **Coconut-Curry Sauce**

Carefully cut the cauliflower and broccoli into small, dime-size pieces. In a medium saucepan, steam all vegetables using coconut water if possible (it will impart a slight sweet flavor). When vegetables are soft and tender but not overly cooked (about 5 minutes), transfer to a bowl and top with Coconut-Curry Sauce. Toss well and add in pomegranate seeds, if desired.

Makes 2 entrée portions.

Butternut-Squash Risotto

Risotto, with its endless possible combinations of vegetables, was a dish that fascinated me during my travels to Italy. This recipe features the fragrance of rosemary, combined with the sweetness of butternut squash. The preparation method is slightly different from that of its traditional Italian counterpart, but the result is the same.

For the risotto:

4 cups steamed Arborio rice

1 tsp. sea salt

For the puree:

2½ cups diced butternut squash

¼ cup extra-virgin olive oil

2 Tbsp. raw honey (optional)

1 clove garlic

2 Tbsp. stemmed fresh rosemary

1 Roma tomato

1 Tbsp. dried basil

½ cup water

In a medium-size bowl, combine rice and sea salt and toss well. Let sit until the rest of the recipe is prepared.

In a high-powered blender, combine all puree ingredients and puree to a smooth consistency. Butternut squash is very dense, so it's important to really work with this mixture until it's rich and creamy. Pour over the rice and toss well. Transfer to a deep baking dish and bake at 250° for 20 minutes. Enjoy garnished with fresh tomato or avocado.

Makes 2 entrée portions.

"Yesterday is history. Tomorrow is a mystery. Today is a gift. That's why we call it 'the present.'"

— AUTHOR UNKNOWN

$\mathcal{L}$IVING IT WELL

The motivation behind the raw-foods lifestyle is largely based on overall health and vitality. "Living it well" can be fun and easy. The road to vibrant health is a journey, and as I've discussed throughout this book, it's important to honor all the steps along the way. Whether you choose to transition to a completely raw diet or integrate more raw meals gracefully into your current lifestyle, you'll derive many rewards from consuming vibrant, wholesome ingredients that really nourish your entire being.

For many clients, starting with a week of living foods can give the body a break from digesting denser meats and cooked starches, provide a quick release of water weight and stored toxins, and stimulate the brain. Here is a suggested guideline for seven days of eating raw that we've implemented successfully with customers of all backgrounds at the 118 restaurant. Consult the shopping list and set aside one or two days in advance to begin putting together your supplies and preparing the basic recipes. That way, this will be a quick, easy, and adventurous process for you!

7 DAYS OF RAW FOODS: A SUGGESTED GUIDE

Shopping and Preparation List for One Person

I recommend shopping for your produce at least twice during the week to keep it really fresh.

FRESH PRODUCE	PANTRY ITEMS	PREPARATION LIST
8 Roma tomatoes	12 cups buckwheat	Apple-Pistachio Granola
4 heirloom tomatoes	14 cups macadamia nuts	Tostadito Shells
18 zucchini	4 cups pistachios	Buckwheat Buns
12 yellow squash	4 cups pumpkin seeds	Focaccia
1 butternut squash	4 cups walnuts	Easy Tortillas
2 portobello mushrooms	16 oz. raw coconut butter	Basic Flax Wraps
10 shiitake mushrooms	2 cups cacao powder	Coconut-Curry Sauce
12 cloves garlic or 2 large bulbs	2 cups Kamut	Hemp Milk
12 cups cleaned spinach	8 oz. tahini paste	Whipped Avocado Spread
2 heads chard	4 cups flaxseed	Smoky Ranchero Sauce
2 heads kale	Chia seeds	Tomatillo Salsa
1 head Napa cabbage	Hemp seeds	Pumpkin-Seed Cheese
6 lemons	Dulse	Chocolate Go-Go Balls
16 oz. strawberries	Maca-root powder	Happy Halvah
4 apples	Dried chipotle peppers	Ice-Cream Slices
6 young Thai coconuts	Extra-virgin olive oil	Berries-'n'-Coconut Yogurt
8 avocados	Flaxseed oil	Macadamia Macaroons
4 cucumbers	Cinnamon	
4 tangerines (mandarin oranges)	Raw honey or raw agave nectar	
Other seasonal fruits and vegetables	Olives (optional)	
	Dates	
	Sea salt	
	Nutmeg	

7-Day Detox Menu

Day 1:

- Apple-Pistachio Granola with Hemp Milk
- Marinated-Kale Deli Salad with Focaccia
- Buddha's Bowl (with sprouted grain)
- Chocolate Go-Go Balls

Day 2:

- Berries-'n'-Coconut Yogurt
- Lemon-Pesto Pasta
- Verde Tacos with Pumpkin-Seed Cheese
- Basic Dessert Bars

Day 3:

- Cacao-Avocado Pudding with fresh strawberries
- Mexi-Cali Chopped Salad
- Strawberry Chard Salad with Buckwheat Buns
- Sunshine Smoothie

Day 4:

- Breakfast Burrito
- Stuffed Heirloom Tomato with Marinated-Shiitake Salad
- Mandarin-Orange Salad with Sprouted-Chia Bread
- Ice-Cream Slices

Day 5:

- Breakfast Bliss Bar
- Chard-Roll Salad
- Chipotle-Ranch Wrap
- Happy Halvah on apples

Day 6:

- Smothered Banana
- Stacked Sweet Noodles
- California Cobb Salad
- Daily 5 Smoothie

Day 7:

- Superfood Smoothie
- "Fried"-Avocado Mini-Tostadas
- Sobeca Sliders
- Macadamia Macaroons

It's very important during this time to follow a health-and-wellness protocol that includes the following:

- 24 oz. of water per day
- Light stretching
- Daily reflection or journaling

Supplement your meals with fresh raw fruits, juices, or basic soups and smoothies to create balance, especially if you exercise heavily.

CLEANSING

Cleansing is a natural part of the healing process and can lead to great results within a brief period of time. You can reverse health disorders, lose weight, rejuvenate your skin, replenish your digestive system, and energize your body in just a few short days while cleansing. Juice or liquid fasting is used in several cultures around the globe, and is recommended two to three times a year to restore health and maintain vitality.

Juicing, in particular, has been used to rejuvenate cells as an enzyme-replacement therapy and has recently had astounding results in treating various forms of cancers and autoimmune disorders. What makes a juice different from, say, a smoothie or blended soup is that the fibers have been removed, leaving a nutrient-dense liquid that can be readily absorbed into the bloodstream and doesn't need to be fully digested. As a result, juices should be enjoyed right away before exposure to the air causes oxidation and begins to diminish the nutritional benefits. Some juicers, such as a Green Star Elite, have advanced extraction methods that actually restructure the juice, making it stable for up to three days in an airtight refrigerated vessel.

The five-day cleanse below has an associated component of learning that is designed to make this an exploration for you, keeping the journey fun and inviting positive experiences for the body and mind.

The 5-Day Liquid Fast

Daily routine:

- 2 blended meals (smoothies or soups)
- At least 1 liter of water
- As much fresh juice as possible, at least 8 oz.

Things to abstain from: coffee, nuts, seeds, avocado, whole and processed foods, dairy and meat products, and refined sugars and starches

Day 1: Intention. Take at least ten minutes today to think about your purpose in doing this cleanse. Write down three to five motivating factors. When you powerfully align with your intention, you're capable of fulfilling these goals and allow yourself the room to grow.

Day 2: Reflection. Take at least ten minutes today to reflect on the things in your life that may be holding you back from reaching your goals or desired way of life. Make a journal entry about these patterns, thoughts, and emotions.

Now sit quietly for three minutes. Close your eyes, envision all of the things you've reflected on, and put all of them inside a box in your mind. Really feel yourself banishing those limiting beliefs or ideas, one by one. You may find it helpful to give each a shape or color, or maybe even a name. My box was full of things such as fear, concerns about others, past failures, and confusion.

Picture yourself in a high, peaceful place (on a mountain or bluff), holding the box in your hands. Then in your mind gently throw it off a cliff, releasing it in peace and feeling gratitude for the lessons it contained. Picture all of those negative things leaving you, and envision pure love and joy filling the spots they used to occupy in your mind and body. Some people describe these feelings visually, as white light or colorful rays. You don't have to know the origin of the radiant energy you feel; you just need to picture it taking the place of the old thoughts.

Day 3: Release. Take some time to stretch today. Any tension your body is holding on to, any fear . . . just release all of it. Remember that your body stores your negative thoughts and emotions, damaging cells in your vital organs and surrounding tissue. It's very natural that during any sort of cleanse, you'll release toxins from these areas into the bloodstream so they may exit the body. During this process, envision a relaxing surrender to your highest possible good.

Day 4: Playfulness. Take some time to be silly today and do something you really love, even if only for five minutes. If you have time to write, journal about how it makes you feel to just play! In the ongoing experience of life, we quite often forget to simply relax and enjoy ourselves. Laughter and the endorphins released during joyful moments support your body in cleansing itself. The daily stress of life continually creates more toxins, so it's important to remember these moments regularly. Reflect on them when you find yourself heading down a negative path, and remind yourself to let go.

Day 5: Celebration. Take a few moments today to pat yourself on the back for all of the good things you bring to the world. Think about your special gifts and offer thanks for them. Call three people you know and thank *them* for the unique ways they make your life better. Journal about what this experience has been like so far, and make some notes about who you want to emerge as when you complete this cleanse. Most important, celebrate your choices this week! Remaining grateful to yourself and your body will help you take the cleanse to the next level in your daily lifestyle.

Recommended Daily Guide to Nutrition While on This Cleanse

— Breakfast. Start the day with a green smoothie or juice. Greens are powerful building blocks and function as brain food. Depending on the day you have ahead of you, it may be a good idea to include some superfoods in your smoothie or juice for added nutrition. (See the Superfood Guide in Chapter 3.)

— **Smoothies as meal replacements.** One to two times a day, you'll be enjoying blended foods. Use the smoothie guide at the beginning of Chapter 3 to help you create fun blends that vary every day, offering balanced nutrition. During the cleansing process, meal-replacement smoothies should be at least 16 oz. and usually not more than 24 oz.

— **Juices.** Suggested combinations include:

- **Apple-lemon-ginger juice:** 2 apples, 1 lemon, and 1 inch fresh ginger root

- **Green juice:** 1 cucumber, 1 cup kale or spinach, 4 celery stalks, and 1 apple

- **Chard-celery juice:** 2 cups chard, 4 stalks celery, ½ cucumber, 1 apple, and ½ lemon

- **Watermelon-cucumber-mint juice:** 2 cups watermelon, 1 cucumber, and 2 Tbsp. fresh mint leaves

- **Pineapple cleanser:** 2 cups pineapple, 1 inch fresh ginger root, and ½ orange

- **Other low-sugar juices**

Other liquids that are acceptable to aid in cleansing: Kombucha, green, and herbal teas

— **Blended soups.** If you love savory foods, I recommend blended soups. Especially during the fall, these recipes are nice because they may be warmed slightly. (See Chapter 6 for soup-warming instructions.)

Celery Miso Soup

¾ cup celery juice

1 clove garlic

1¼ cups water

1 tsp. Himalayan salt

1 Tbsp. miso paste

1 stalk green onion

2 Tbsp. extra-virgin olive oil

Tomato Bisque

2 Roma tomatoes
1 clove garlic
1 cup water
1 tsp. Himalayan salt
1 Tbsp. Italian herbs

Simple Gazpacho

2 Roma tomatoes
½ cucumber
1 red bell pepper
¼ cup extra-virgin olive oil or flaxseed oil
1 tsp. sea salt
Herbs to taste

Basic Vegetable Soup

1 zucchini
1 tomato
1 red bell pepper
1 cup celery juice
1 clove garlic
1 tsp. sea salt
1 dash cayenne pepper

Sea-Me Soup

¼ cup laver (soaked; use water in recipe)
1 zucchini
¼ cup dulse
1 clove garlic
1 tsp. sea salt
2 Tbsp. extra-virgin olive oil
1 Tbsp. miso paste

For all soups, blend ingredients in a basic blender until well combined. Enjoy within 2 days.

Makes 1 serving each.

10 Ways to Incorporate
Living Foods into a Daily Diet

After any cleansing process, it's easier to jump into living foods, as your body is craving more of the same fresh, vital energy. Here are some tips to keep in mind on your journey to incorporate more of this cuisine into your daily diet using the recipes in this book:

1. **Supergreen smoothies:** Start your day with a delicious smoothie blended with fresh fruit, greens, and superfoods!

2. **Salads:** Have a salad with every meal. Fresh greens aid digestion and provide chlorophyll to help break down the proteins in the food you eat.

3. **Vivacious wraps:** Collard greens, red chard, and romaine lettuce can all be wrapped around fresh vegetables, hummus, guacamole, and more. This is a nice alternative to a salad.

4. **Superfoods = super you!:** There are several raw superfoods available as supplements. Add these vital nutrients to salads, sandwiches, pastas, and wraps. Because much produce is cultivated in depleted soils, adding the vitamins and minerals from superfoods can help remedy basic health concerns such as low hormone levels, chronic fatigue, concentration issues, an unbalanced metabolism, and arthritis. These are all attributed to demineralization in the body.

5. **Juices:** Especially for people with busy schedules, fresh juices can be a lifesaver. Apple, orange, and pineapple juices hold their enzyme content throughout the day and act as preservatives in fruit and vegetable blends. Sip on an apple-lemon-ginger blast and *feel* the amazing energy (it really is better than coffee!).

6. **Dark, leafy greens:** Add kale, spinach, chard, or collards to your next sandwich. Remember that just adding more of the "good stuff" can jump-start your health and take it to the next level.

7. **Fruit salads for dessert:** If you have a sweet tooth, try fresh fruit salads for dessert. Make them fun by using different ingredients such as coconut, cherimoya, sapote, pineapple, mango, and fresh berries! These are a fast and easy solution when you don't have time to whip up a more advanced raw dessert.

8. **Raw ice creams:** These delicious desserts can be made in advance and enjoyed at the end of a meal or as a high-protein snack. The essential fatty acids serve as a sustained source of fuel for the body . . . and you'll be treating yourself to a vital, vibrant meal at the same time.

9. **Breakfast delight:** If you're a breakfast lover, enjoy this meal any time of the day. Raw breakfast items (see Chapter 3), although oftentimes sweet, are very high in protein. Try a delicious banana smothered in almond butter instead of a candy bar for your midday snack.

10. **Squash pastas:** Squash pastas are a fantastic quick fix and can be easily tossed with your favorite fruits and vegetables, as well as a variety of sauces. They make a great alternative to the standard salad and, of course, to the heaviness of a regular pasta dish. You can begin by simply substituting the noodles and leaving the rest of the ingredients in your favorite pasta recipe, and then slowly adapting your selections as your body calls for more vibrant foods.

AFTERWORD

"Take the first step in faith. You don't have to see the whole staircase, just take the first step."

— ATTRIBUTED TO DR. MARTIN LUTHER KING, JR.

Beginning to incorporate living foods into your diet can be as easy as adding Hemp Milk to your coffee, or replacing your breakfast with a Daily 5 Smoothie. This can be a process of exploration as you learn to enjoy new flavors and textures, sticking with the items you enjoy the most and making them a staple in your home. Adding more of the "good stuff" will leave less room for the "other stuff" in your diet. Your cravings will begin to shift, and your body really will lead the way to more wholesome choices to follow.

Whether you're compelled to try these new recipes in your own quest for vibrant health or for the sake of your family's, you'll reap immense rewards across the board as your body uses this nourishment to help you achieve your deepest desires and goals. When I stumbled upon living foods in *my* quest for health, I wasn't committed to the lifestyle from the very first moment I heard about it. Rather, I remained open to trying something new and taking baby steps. After just a week of raw foods, I was convinced that this lifestyle could help heal me physically and mentally and bring me closer to the true essence of the person I was, body and mind.

This was where my commitment to a healthier life began, and the journey since that time has been all about sharing what I've learned with extended family and friends who are in their own way seeking solutions or a pathway to more vibrant living. I hope this book takes the mystery out of living foods and the associated lifestyle, and helps inspire *you* to choose more of the good stuff in your own daily diet. May you enjoy vibrant health in every way!

—Jenny Ross

$\mathcal{A}$PPENDIX A:

GARNISHES

What to do with your leftovers? Here is a basic guide to dehydrating some basic garnishes using the leftovers from recipes in this book.

FRUIT AND VEGETABLE GARNISHES

Fruits and vegetable leftovers, as well as herbs, can be dehydrated straight on a dehydrator tray. (It's best to cut them down into thin pieces.) Dehydrate at 118° for 10–12 hours until completely dry. Herbs can be ground into dried seasonings; vegetables, too, can be ground into a powder, or saved as whole pieces for a festive plating decoration. Fruits may be kept in an airtight container, and are perfect for long hikes or snacks on the run.

MARINATED-VEGETABLE GARNISHES

Marinated vegetables can be completely dehydrated to create a savory topping for salads and soups. Just set the dehydrator at 118° and dehydrate for up to 15 hours, until the vegetables are crispy and dry. Be sure to place only a thin layer on the dehydrator tray; and when tomatoes and peppers are involved, rotate every 4 hours to prevent fermentation on any of the sides.

NUT AND SEED GARNISHES

Leftover nut and seed cheeses may be spread in a thin layer over a covered dehydrator tray and dehydrated at 118° for up to 15 hours. These dried cheeses make a great crumble to serve over soups, salads, and entrées. Store these dried toppings indefinitely in airtight containers. It's best to keep them removed from moisture to prevent condensation or mold.

BASIC MARINATED NUTS AND SEEDS

To create basic marinated nuts and seeds, begin by soaking the ingredients for 4–8 hours. Afterward, rinse and drain off soak water. Then in a mixing bowl, coat the nuts or seeds lightly in olive oil, adding a mixture of fresh or dried herbs (try chili powder, sea salt, and 1 tsp. honey for a sweet and spicy blend). Place on a covered dehydrator tray and dehydrate at 118° for 15 hours. Rotate twice during the drying cycle so that all sides are evenly exposed to warm air. Store in an airtight container and enjoy throughout the week!

Appendix B:

LIVING-BODY SOURCES OF NUTRITION

When you're considering a lifestyle shift or dealing with health issues, knowing plant-based sources of nutrition can be helpful. It's important to find balance in your weekly diet, so use this guide as a reference to be sure these nutrients are well represented among your food choices.

- **Iron:** Yams; sea vegetables; dark, leafy greens; tahini; green superfoods

- **B vitamins:** Green superfoods; sea vegetables

- **Protein and amino acids:** Dark, leafy greens (kale, mustard greens, collard greens, romaine, spinach, chard); nuts and seeds (flax, chia, almonds); mushrooms (shiitake, maitake, enoki, cremini, portobello); broccoli; sea vegetables; sprouted grains (buckwheat, Kamut, rye, wheat berries); green superfoods (chlorella, E$_3$Live, spirulina, other green powders); maca-root powder (contains all amino acids)

- **Essential fats:** Seeds (flax, hemp, chia); avocados; olives (including olive oil); coconuts; nuts (macadamia nuts, walnuts, pecans, Brazil nuts); cacao

- **Fiber:** All squashes; eggplant; greens; bananas; sprouted grains; flaxseed; psyllium husk; apples; pears; pineapples; melons; buckwheat; quinoa

- **Other vitamins and minerals:** All plant foods (especially heirloom varieties); all superfoods

REFERENCES

Amen, D. *Magnificent Mind at Any Age: Natural Ways to Unleash Your Brain's Maximum Potential*. New York: Three Rivers Press, 2009.

Balch, P. *Prescription for Nutritional Healing*. 4th Edition. New York: Penguin, 2006.

Baroody, T. *Alkalize or Die*. 8th Edition. Waynesville, NC: Holographic Health Inc., 1991.

Boutenko, V. *Green for Life*. Ashland, OR: Raw Family Publishing, 2005.

Campbell, M. J.; and Koeffler, P. Toward therapeutic intervention of cancer by vitamin D compounds. *Journal of the National Cancer Institute*. 1997. 89(3): 182–185.

Cleland, L. G.; and James, M. J. Rheumatoid arthritis and the balance of dietary N-6 and N-3 essential fatty acids. *Br J Rheumatol*. 1997. May 36(5): 513–514.

Clemente, A. Enzymatic protein hydrolysates in human nutrition. *Trends Food Sci Tech*. 2000. 11: 254–262.

Clementz, G. L.; and Schade, S. G. The spectrum of vitamin B_{12} deficiency. *Am Fam Physician*. 1990. Jan 41(1): 150–162.

Colditz, G. A.; Manson, J. E; et al. Diet and risk of clinical diabetes in women. *Am J Clin Nutr*. 1992. May 55(5): 1018–1023.

Connor, S. L.; and Connor, W. E. Are fish oils beneficial in the prevention and treatment of coronary artery disease. *Am J Clin Nutr*. 1997. Oct 66(4 Suppl): 1020S–1031S.

Cook, J. D.; Dassenko, S. A.; Whittaker, P. Calcium supplementation: effect on iron absorption. *Am J Clin Nutr*. 1991. 53: 106–111.

Cousens, G. *Rainbow Green Live-Food Cuisine*. Berkeley, CA: North Atlantic Books, 2003.

Dalton, L. What is that stuff? Food preservatives. *Chemical and Engineering News*. 2002. Nov 80: 44.

Dietary Reference Intakes for Energy, Carbohydrate, Fiber, Fat, Fatty Acids, Cholesterol, Protein, and Amino Acids. Food and Nutrition Board. Institute of Medicine. Washington, D.C.: National Academies Press, 2002: 423.

Dietary Reference Intakes for Vitamin C, Vitamin E, Selenium and Caroteinoids. Food and Nutrition Board. Institute of Medicine. Washington, D.C.: National Academies Press, 2000: 343–344.

Domingo, J. L. Health risks of genetically modified foods: Many opinions but few data. *Science.* 2000. 288: 1748–1749.

García-Casal, M. N.; Pereira, A. C.; Leets, I.; et al. High iron content and bioavailability in humans from four species of marine algae. *J Nutr.* 2007. 137: 2691–2695.

Jubb, D.; and Jubb, A. *Lifefood Recipe Book: Living on Life Force.* Berkeley, CA: North Atlantic Books, 2003.

Krishnaiah, D.; Rosalam, S.; Prasad, D. M. R.; et al. Mineral content of some seaweeds from Sabah's South China Sea. *Asian J Scientific Res.* 2008. 1: 166–170.

Kuiper, H. A.; Noteborn, H. P. J. M.; and Peijnenburg, A. A. C. M. Adequacy of methods for testing the safety of genetically modified foods. *The Lancet.* 1999. 354: 1315–1316.

McBride, J. Can Foods Forestall Aging? *Agricultural Research.* 1999. 47(2): 15–17.

Morse, R. *Detox Miracle Sourcebook.* Prescott, AZ: Hohm Press, 2004.

Murray, M. *The Encyclopedia of Healing Foods.* New York: Atria Books, 2005.

Pfeiffer, E. *Soil Fertility, Renewal and Preservation: Bio-Dynamic Farming and Gardening.* Delhi, India: Asiatic Publishing House, 2006.

Prior, R.; Hoang, H.; Gu, L.; Bacchiocca, M.; Howard, L.; Hanpsch-Woodill, M.; Huang, D.; Ou, B.; and Jacob, R. Assays for hydrophilic and lipophilic antioxidant capacity of plasma and other biological and food samples. *Journal of Agricultural and Food Chemistry.* 2003. 51: 3273–3279.

Steinbrecher, A; and Linseisen, J. Dietary intake of individual glucosinolates in participants of the EPIC-Heidelberg Cohort Study. *Ann Nutr Metab.* 2009. 54: 87–96.

Wu, X.; Beecher, G.; Holden, J.; Haytowitz, D.; Gebhardt, S.; and Prior, R. Lipophilic and hydrophilic antioxidant capacities of common foods in the United States. *Journal of Agricultural and Food Chemistry.* 2004. 52: 4026–4037.

About the Author

Jenny Ross is a raw-food chef and the CEO of Creative Blend, a company that produces and distributes raw-food meals called Jenny Ross Living Foods at health-food stores throughout the country. She's the culinary creator of 118 Degrees, the premier Orange County raw restaurant, which is continually filled with happy customers from all walks of life. A former model, Jenny discovered raw food in 1999 in her own personal quest to enjoy vibrant health, and she learned how to prepare it by studying with raw-food chefs from around the world. Afterward, she realized her passion to share the journey of healthful eating with others and began working with living foods professionally in the year 2000.

Jenny regularly gives speeches and interviews about raw foods, teaches raw-food-preparation classes, and is a certified health coach. She's appeared on *G Word* on the Discovery Channel; Travel Channel's *Taste of America* program; and Channels 5, 7, and 9 in Los Angeles. Jenny was honored as a Hot 25 influential business leader in Orange County in 2008 by *OC Metro*, and was dubbed the "Sexiest Chef" in Orange County in 2007 by *Riviera* magazine.

Website: **www.118degrees.com**

RECIPE INDEX

We hope you enjoyed this Hay House book. If you'd like to receive our online
catalog featuring additional information on Hay House books and products, or
if you'd like to find out more about the Hay Foundation, please contact:

Hay House, Inc., P.O. Box 5100, Carlsbad, CA 92018-5100
(760) 431-7695 or (800) 654-5126
(760) 431-6948 (fax) or (800) 650-5115 (fax)
www.hayhouse.com® • **www.hayfoundation.org**

Published and distributed in Australia by: Hay House Australia Pty. Ltd., 18/36 Ralph St.,
Alexandria NSW 2015 • *Phone:* 612-9669-4299 • *Fax:* 612-9669-4144 • www.hayhouse.com.au

Published and distributed in the United Kingdom by: Hay House UK, Ltd., 292B Kensal Rd.,
London W10 5BE • *Phone:* 44-20-8962-1230 • *Fax:* 44-20-8962-1239 • www.hayhouse.co.uk

Published and distributed in the Republic of South Africa by: Hay House SA (Pty), Ltd., P.O. Box 990,
Witkoppen 2068 • *Phone/Fax:* 27-11-467-8904 • www.hayhouse.co.za

Published in India by: Hay House Publishers India, Muskaan Complex, Plot No. 3, B-2, Vasant Kunj,
New Delhi 110 070 • *Phone:* 91-11-4176-1620 • *Fax:* 91-11-4176-1630 • www.hayhouse.co.in

Distributed in Canada by: Raincoast, 9050 Shaughnessy St., Vancouver, B.C. V6P 6E5
Phone: (604) 323-7100 • *Fax:* (604) 323-2600 • www.raincoast.com

Take Your Soul on a Vacation

Visit **www.HealYourLife.com**® to regroup, recharge, and reconnect
with your own magnificence. Featuring blogs, mind-body-spirit news,
and life-changing wisdom from Louise Hay and friends.

Visit **www.HealYourLife.com** today!